CW00460923

the

PUNISHED

the

PUNISHED

STORIES OF DEATH-ROW PRISONERS IN INDIA

BASED
ON
WORK BY
PROJECT
39A

jahnavi misra

HarperCollins *Publishers* India

First published in India by
HarperCollins *Publishers* in 2021
A-75, Sector 57, Noida, Uttar Pradesh 201301, India
www.harpercollins.co.in

2 4 6 8 10 9 7 5 3 1

P-ISBN: 978-93-9035-187-9
E-ISBN: 978-93-9035-188-6

Typeset in 12/16.2 Galliard BT at
Manipal Technologies Limited, Manipal

Illustrations by Aparajita Ninan

Printed and bound at
Thomson Press (India) Ltd

Foreword

THE Death Penalty Researh Project at National Law University, Delhi interviewed nearly 400 prisoners sentenced to death and their families between 2013-16. Nothing could have prepared me for the experience of interviewing death-row prisoners and sitting in those dark, oppressive prisons across different parts of India. I realised that my decade-long legal education had not prepared me for the sheer force of the human experience that I was witnessing. No amount of intellectual sophistication could have equipped me to deal with the raw emotion of hundreds of prisoners constantly swinging between the hope for life and the fear of death. It is hard to explain those settings – the sense of expectation, the stark hopelessness and the cruel reality of incessantly anticipating one's own death. The researcher is a curious being in the midst of all this.

Giving effect to the permissions from 'higher ups', prisoners sentenced to death were told to talk to us by prison officials and didn't really have the choice to refuse. As researchers, we were strangers suddenly prying into the darkest aspects of their lives, asking them to immediately trust us with their innermost feelings of anger, frustration, shame, fear, hope and everything else in between. Against the ticking clock set by prison officials, we were invariably in a tearing hurry to open up their lives, making them relive some of their most traumatic episodes, only to suddenly disappear after having documented what we wanted.

Across different prisons, death-row prisoners almost always saw us as people who had come from 'Delhi' with the power and the resources to alter their fates. The guilt of knowing their interest in talking to us and our inability to help even in the smallest measure was often overwhelming. In those moments of expectation, to repeatedly tell them that we could not offer any kind of legal assistance and to choose research ethics over addressing their suffering was a demanding moral burden. All that we had to offer in return was taking their stories and suffering to the outside world. We were repeatedly asked if our research would help them, only for us to convey our embarrassment and helplessness by saying that we couldn't be sure. In many ways they understood that their stories would speak to a future time, and that they themselves might be in no position to benefit from it.

Even in courtrooms, they are often defined by their crimes alone and very little else. Despite the law requiring that a much broader canvas about their lives be considered during sentencing, their stories barely ever enter the courtroom. Hamstrung by their poverty and inability to afford effective legal representation, their stories are neither presented nor demanded in any real sense. The silence about their lives is only louder in the public conversation on the death penalty. Given the crimes in question, the shrillness of public discourse reduces the death-row prisoner to one event in their lives. It is almost as though we are afraid to find out anything more making it a ritualistic necessity that we first dehumanise a person before executing them. These stories are an attempt to shatter that moral simplicity and comfort, and present death-row prisoners as individuals with complicated inner lives.

An equally important part of the project was to interview the families of death-row prisoners. In awarding and executing death sentences, the public imagination has very little space to consider the pain being inflicted on the family members of the prisoner. Given the tremendous public pressure in these cases, the families of death-row prisoners end up leading an immensely vulnerable and alienated life. Poverty, social boycott, ridicule and threats of violence are all tragic realities of their lives. They are people everyone forgets. I assume we tuck them away in some corner of our mind as the unfortunate but, perhaps, necessary cost for the retributive justice that we seek.

Our work after the Death Penalty India Report has involved providing pro bono representation to prisoners sentenced to death. As part of that representation, we carry out what are called 'mitigation investigations' to reconstruct the lives of prisoners in order to present it in court as sentencing information for judges to consider. Compared to the limitations of the single-conversation format of the Death Penalty Research Project, mitigaton investigations have a much longer and deeper arc with many more conversations with the prisoner, their family members, friends, colleagues, partners and acquaintances. Building trust and confidence for people to talk about their lives without the fear of being judged or abandoned is a time consuming process. But at the end of that process, what often emerge are narratives of people whose lives go farther than single incidents in their lives.

While the Death Penalty India Report published in May 2016 was an academic endeavour based on these interviews, this collection of stories is an effort to bring the complex realities of their stories to a much larger audience. I have no illusions about these stories convincing people to oppose the death penalty. That is a longer and more arduous task. These stories are meant to put forward a human understanding of those we condemn to a life of misery, suffering and pain.

All of us at Project 39A and National Law University, Delhi cannot thank Jahnavi enough for transforming our research into the profoundly moving stories you will read in this book. It was inspiring to see the stories break out from the confines of academic writing. None of this research would have been possible without the massive contributions of the student researchers at National Law University, Delhi. Meeting prisoners and their families while listening to stories challenged and moved them profoundly and has deeply influenced their thinking about the role of law in our society.

Since we conducted these interviews, we have lost some of the prisoners to illnesses in prison, death by suicide and the ultimate aim of the death penalty – death by hanging. Some of them have been acquitted and released and some had their death sentences commuted to life in prison, but many continue to live under the shadow of the death penalty. The stories in this volume are written with the hope of making readers understand the people we want to kill. It is as much about the lives of prisoners and their families as it is about holding a mirror to society. Ultimately, it is an appeal to the humanity in all of us to know a little more about the people whose lives we want to take.*

Anup Surendranath
November, 2020
Delhi

---

* All names and identifying details in the stories have been changed to protect the privacy of individuals.

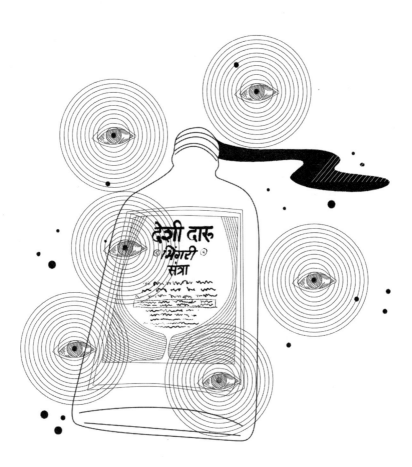

Confessions of a Father

WE all sat down on the floor of their hut. The mother wiped her tears and said that she could not bear to hear her husband's ramblings, and left on an errand. The father was free to say what he wanted. 'Tell us what happened that night,' we asked.

'The policemen barged into our home and said, "Come with us right now!" My elder son insisted that we did not know where Rajni was, but they shoved and kicked us till we got into the van. The nasha that was supposed to get me through the night left my body so quickly that it felt like the twenty rupees and two hours I had spent drinking that evening had only been a dream. When we got to the police station, we saw that my daughters' husbands had been picked up from their homes too. I will not lie, seeing them there was a bit of a relief. But then the beatings started.

"Tell us where he is!", the policemen yelled as they lashed us with lathis. Even my wife received a couple of slaps. "It is wrong to beat us like this. We have not done anything wrong," the stupid woman kept repeating.

'In my heart I really cursed Rajni at that time, both for the beating and for that night's wasted drink money. It's a good thing that the cheap, local liquor has made my body weak; I passed out quickly. When I regained consciousness, I found out that one of my sons-in-law had lost his hearing because of the beating. Rajni surrendered soon after just to save us from the police.

It is good to talk about it with someone. I am very happy that you have decided to interview me. Nobody else speaks to me anymore. If I had been a younger man, then maybe my family would have taken me more seriously; now they just think of me as a useless drunk. You are very smart to think of talking to me.'

'Do you know what your son is in jail for?' we asked.

'People say it is a very sensitive case because the girl who was raped and murdered was only seven or eight years old,' he replied. 'These people are using Rajni's case as a lesson for others. Rajni is my youngest son and I used to think that he was only twelve, but my wife says that he is probably around twenty. Maybe an old image of him as a little boy is still stuck in my head.'

'There is only circumstantial evidence against your son,' we pointed out. 'Apparently someone saw him walking with the girl. Do you believe that your son is guilty?'

'Rajni says that he is innocent. My wife says that he is innocent. Many people believe that he has been framed.

The lawyers don't tell us anything. Nobody in the family is educated enough to understand all this legal stuff. If you ask me, I really don't know if he has done it or not. All I know is that although the blessed liquor allows me to laugh my worries away, my son's pain hits me from time to time. I am not able to stop crying when that happens. Sometimes I cry even as I'm laughing.

'My son is lost, but my wife does not allow me to go and visit him because she thinks that I might not be able to make my way back home. I know what Rajni is going through despite not having seen him in many years. I think alcohol has given me this special gift where I can sense the pain of my loved ones even when I am not with them.'

'Does your wife really stop you from visiting your son?'

'My wife does not understand. She thinks of me only as a drunken idiot; another liability in her already grief-stricken life. She feels ashamed because the neighbours laugh at me. But in reality, she is the one who is stupid. She sold our land to pay for this good-for-nothing lawyer; she thought he was competent because his name was in the newspaper. He did not do anything to save our son. People say that he did not even produce the reports of the medical examination in court. We barely have enough money to eat now and my wife blames my drinking, but the truth is that it is she who has wasted the little we had on useless lawyers.'

'You cried when we said that your son is doing well, and has even learnt to write his name in prison. Why?'

'I cried because I did not know how to convey the sadness I felt on hearing that. I never encouraged my children to study. I don't even know how many years any of them spent in school. Rajni had to go to jail to learn to write. I was never sent to school by my parents, so I thought I did not need to send my children either. But in today's times, it is important to be able to read and write. Sometimes I feel that Rajni's fate might have been different had I forced him to study.'

'Can we ask when you started drinking?'

'Can't say for sure, but I think I must have been around twenty. I got married to Rajni's mother when I was eighteen or nineteen, and we had children soon after. I used to work hard and alcohol helped me relax. But my family is very ungrateful. They resent the fact that I need to retire now. How much will I work? Now it is their turn. Drinking is not a crime. And still my family accuses me of bringing them more shame than even Rajni. They are all against me. I might as well go and kill myself right now. Talking to you all so much is making me dizzy. Leave me alone!'

He got up from the floor with difficulty and zigzagged his way to the door. At the threshold, he turned around and said, 'What a bunch of fools!' Then he walked into the dark. We continued to hear his humming till he disappeared. We could not have left their hut unlocked, so we had to wait for half an hour for the mother to return before we left.

How Chanda Became the Gurumata

A s soon as Chanda was brought back to prison, her friends ran to her and embraced her, sobbing a little. The others in the TV room looked at her sadly. Chanda had spent four years in prison waiting for the hearing and had finally been called to court that day. The verdict had been pronounced.

'Twenty years is a long time, I know,' she said to the women. 'My rotten luck.'

'What are you talking about?' they asked. 'We just saw the news. You've been given the death penalty.'

It was as though a truck suddenly, inaudibly, rammed into Chanda's insides. Her ears rang in a manner that had become all too familiar. She controlled herself. 'Accha?

Lawyer saab and my husband said I got twenty years. Who knows what they keep babbling in English.' Her two best friends, Kalpana and Asha, rubbed her back to calm her.

———•———

'The tantric gurumata, Chanda Kumari, wanted to attain siddhi through the gruesome sacrifice of a two-year-old boy,' they had repeatedly announced on TV. Chanda almost smiled as she thought about it later that night. They had made her seem important. The last time that she had felt important was when she was sixteen and had given birth to her first son. People had looked at her with approval then; now they looked at her with revulsion. Not in the prison, though – they were all sisters there. She liked to imagine that the women were like a group of tainted widows, each driven there by their own catastrophic fate, sapped of life and placed atop a neatly arranged ritualistic pyre; human sacrifice being a long-standing tradition. Little did anyone realize that the tainted widows slowly regained strength and lifeblood amongst each other.

Chanda tried to meditate. She had become good at it in the past few months. But whenever she closed her eyes tonight, the memory of that beautiful evening, her relatives congratulating her on bearing a son, kept coming back to her. The dead boy must have been a beloved son too. She knew that his name was Kuldeep – the light at the end of a long, probably murky, tunnel of ancestral history.

'What has happened has happened,' she chanted and tried to still her mind by pushing out all disturbing thoughts, but it wasn't to be. Not tonight. When she lay down and closed her eyes again, she saw her legs dangling like in Bollywood movies – hanged till death. She opened her eyes again, tried once more to meditate, and so the night passed.

She got up at four in the morning and performed her usual puja. She used to do puja at home too, but now she made sure that it consumed the entirety of her mornings. Then she sat down with the day's quota of rice and carefully sifted through it. That was her job in prison. She examined each grain as if her life depended on it.

'Come sit with us, Chanda,' invited Kalpana on her way to the TV room. She quietly watched Kalpana and Asha laughing and joking, as though they never thought about the crimes they had committed. It struck Chanda for the first time that the reason the two got along well was because they had both done the same thing – killed their husbands. Would she have done it too had she known that she would end up in prison anyway, she wondered.

Their favourite soap opera, full of romance and pathos, was playing on TV. Chanda liked it a lot – the hero was a strikingly handsome young man, and the heroine very pretty. But since she had learnt about the death penalty, her past life kept flashing before her eyes, distracting her.

Twenty-five years prior, her alcoholic father had got her married at the age of thirteen. She was saddled with a tantric witch doctor for a husband, Pawan Kumar, and taken from one hellhole to another. At least there had been enough to eat. Her husband's jhaad-phoonk exorcism had earned him his family's scorn, but also some money. How strange her life was then – barely able to speak, sticking to the walls of that tiny house like an emaciated ghost.

She remembered clearly the night that she became involved in the madness. Her husband was squatting in a corner, stuck to his chillum like a calf to an udder. He'd had a long day of waving his peacock-feathered broom in people's faces to cure them of illnesses ranging from fever to depression. Chanda cooked in silence, dreading her husband's nightly hurling of overdone rotis or underdone potatoes. But that night he seemed uninterested in the food. Instead he looked at her and said, 'You too should dedicate yourself to this work. Together we could have an army of followers.'

Chanda wasn't too keen at first, but the more interest she showed – fetching him things for his rituals or pretending to listen to his ramblings – the less her husband cared about burnt rotis. He soon started accepting disciples, and they eventually had a group of five men keen to learn tantric mysticism from them. Her husband became the guru and she became the gurumata. It was only five men then, but the whole world knew her as the tantric gurumata.

Chanda was barely able to follow the soap blaring on the TV when she was called from the room. Her sister had come to visit her.

'Don't worry, didi,' her sister said, 'I met Pawan jeeja before coming here. He said that the lawyer will appeal in the high court.'

'How is he?' Chanda asked quietly.

'Who? Pawan jeeja? He is good.'

Chanda knew that her whole family hated him. She was surprised that her sister had gone to visit him.

'He said that he had already told you that the sentence can get commuted to twenty years,' her sister said.

'Oh . . . is that what they were trying to tell me?' muttered Chanda to herself. 'How are the children?' she asked.

'It has been difficult,' her sister replied. 'They don't go out to play or anything . . . they just stay at home. But all will be okay soon, I'm sure.'

No, Chanda thought. She was born a prisoner, and she would die in prison, amongst her friends – maybe a little less of a prisoner.

The visit was short. Chanda returned to the TV room, looking forward to the next day's routine.

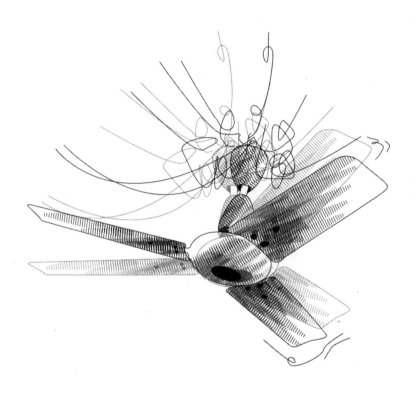

Contempt of Court

THE fan was so slow and squeaky that at times Jameel Qureshi could only hear its swishing and swooshing, instead of the arguments presented by the lawyers. He had to really strain to listen and to understand things, and even then he managed to miss many important points. There were moments when his brain would get so overwhelmed that it would involuntarily focus on the sounds of the fan. These moments lulled him into a stupor.

Drifting into oblivion was easier than fighting, but he forced himself to pay attention – not so much because he wanted to escape the death penalty, but because he wanted a chance to speak, in case it was allowed. He was almost beyond the fear of death now. All he wanted was a chance to talk, and he got it in the end.

'May I please say something before the judgment is pronounced?' he asked the judge, ignoring his lawyer's apprehensive glances.

The judge took off his reading glasses. He looked at the defendant and said, 'I am obliged to let you speak under statement 313. Go ahead, what do you want to say?'

'Thank you, sir,' Jameel said, adjusting his black shirt and clearing his throat. 'I just want to say that the police dragged me from city to city. They tried me for previous charges and current charges, and scrutinized the record of every person that I have ever met to try and form a good picture of future charges. I know you will say that it is good policing, but how does it justify all the times they made connections where there weren't any, just to prove their own preconceived theories? The fact of the matter is that the police does not like me, so here I am standing in front of you for a crime I have not committed.'

The judge was not impressed. 'Mr Qureshi, state clearly whatever you want to say in your defence.'

'But sir, how can I defend myself in a situation where scrutiny has turned into narrow-minded obsession? The police worked hard on this case, but their work has not been completely above board.'

'Do you understand what is happening here?' the judge asked. 'Farrukh Siddiqui confessed to planning the attack and took your name in relation to the said attack.'

'The police arrested many of us, sir. Farrukh was the only one who confessed. And that was not because he had anything to do with the attack, but because we were badly beaten up by the police. He probably could not take it anymore,' said Jameel Qureshi.

'Your lawyer has gone through all of this with us, Mr Qureshi. The fact remains that there is no evidence that the confession was made under duress,' the judge stated.

'Is it okay then for them to have pointed a gun at me and ordered me to confess? Is it okay for them to have denied me a lawyer during the interrogation? They even harassed my family and warned my sister against visiting me,' Jameel blurted out.

'Do not lose your cool in this court. There is no proof of any of this. I think you should stop talking if you've had your say,' the judge said, putting his reading glasses back on.

'But,' Jameel burst out again, 'all the proof and evidence that was produced during these hearings was only what the police wanted you to see, sir. Early in the interrogation, they had asked me to hand over my watch. A few months later, I saw it being produced as evidence. They even made me sign a blank paper once.'

'The police did its job, Mr Qureshi. Do not undermine the impact of that attack on the national conscience,' said the judge sternly.

'But then what is the difference, sir?' Jameel Qureshi asked, his desperation becoming more and more apparent. 'What is the difference between those who are criticized for killing innocent people in the name of politics and religion and the police? How are their actions justified? I have not only seen them planting false evidence, but also torturing innocent people. Is that okay just because it is for the benefit of national defence?'

'You have the gall to compare the police force to terrorist organizations?' the judge almost screamed.

'No sir. I am just telling you what is in my heart. I have only had some basic education, so I might not be saying the right things. But I am able to say what I want because I have nothing to lose; in any case, I will probably be hanged or kept in jail for a long time. There is no sense in being afraid any more. I also want to add, sir, that there are many rules and regulations, but nobody really follows them.'

The judge quickly wrote something on the large book in front of him, and got ready to pronounce his judgement.

The sound of the fan started to seem loud again, and Jameel let his mind focus on the lulling swishing and swooshing. He had said what he wanted to say, nothing else mattered anymore.

Fast Track to Justice

'TELL us your name again,' the policeman screamed.

'Sanjeev Sharma,' the man replied as if from far, far away, his mouth swollen and bloody.

'Why did you do that to the little girl?' the policeman asked.

'I don't know, sahib. I did not,' replied Sanjeev, as another blow landed on his ear. 'Tweeeeeeee,' his ears rang for some time.

'How could you do something so disgusting?' the policeman was screaming when his hearing returned.

'I am sorry, sahib,' Sanjeev said with the little air still left in his lungs.

'So you did do it, didn't you?' the policeman asked.

'I must have, sahib. You can't be wrong,' Sanjeev said and passed out. The policeman's work was done. Sanjeev was left alone after that.

———•———

The next thing Sanjeev remembered was the police dragging him into court. A lot of press had gathered, and all the screaming and shouting confused him further. Somebody pushed him inside and the proceedings began. The proceedings were conducted entirely in English. The fact that he could not understand a word was scary for a while, but then it just became plain boring. Then the dread returned every time someone looked at him, and then the boredom set in again as soon as they started talking amongst themselves. These two alternating emotions hit him in such strong waves that by the end of it he wanted to vomit.

From the court, he was taken back to a cell in the police station. He was given a bowl of thin dal and some gritty rice that he ate quickly. He was struck by how utterly dark the cell became at night. The onset of night also brought an onslaught of mosquitoes, which kept him up till the morning. He tried his best to come to terms with whatever was going on, but every sensation was so sudden and so strong that his brain was not able to process anything.

He was dragged to court again the next day. The same fear, the same boredom and the same confusion. Then back to the dark cell.

By the third day, he had gone completely numb. He saw the lawyers and the judge confer in court, but could not hear anything. He felt as though he was floating and watching a film form above without any audio. Then the judge uttered the words, 'hanged till death'. He might not have known English, but something about those words was so stark that they did not require translation. He re-entered his body; the confusion vanished and understanding dawned. Finally, he knew what to feel. Fear.

The press was in an even greater frenzy when Sanjeev was brought out after the sentencing on the third day. 'Fast-track court pronounces the verdict in just three days!' they screamed into their mikes and cameras from every side. 'The case of the rape and murder of four-year-old Meeta has been closed in just three days. Justice has been served!'

As I write this, it has been ten months since that day. Sanjeev is in prison awaiting execution. The food in prison is as bad as it was at the police station on those first few nights, and the mosquitoes continue to relish his blood more than anyone else's. Press interest in the case has continued because of the quick verdict, so he has been giving many interviews to journalists and human rights activists. His biggest predicament is that he does not really know how to answer their questions. He invariably disappoints everyone who talks to him.

They ask him whether reports of the medical examination were produced in court. He is not sure about that. He doesn't even remember if a medical examination had in fact been conducted. They ask him whether he was assigned a good lawyer and if his case was represented well. He does not know – he did not understand anything since it was all in English. And how is he to know if the lawyer was good or bad when he never actually spoke to him. Sometimes they ask him if he put in an appeal to the high court. He does not know about any such process, nor is he aware of how to go about filing an appeal. The trickiest question that he has ever been asked is whether he thinks justice has been done in his case. He does not know that either.

All he does know is that one day he was in police custody, and by the third he had received a death sentence. All he knows is that he is poor, so he can't really do anything about it. All he knows is that he hates the thin dal and the dry rotis he is given to eat every day, and most of all he hates the mosquitoes that suck his blood and refuse to let him sleep even for an hour or two at night.

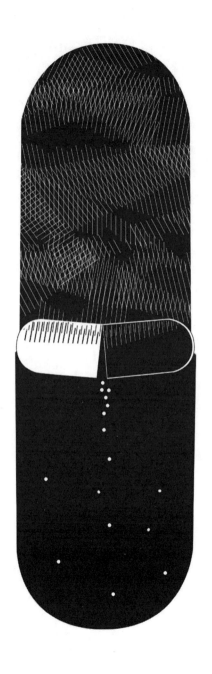

Prashant Bhave's Madness

'HE was a madman! Went and rammed the bus into a bunch of people. All for what, a few days of leave?' yelled Prashant Bhave's employer. 'It's good that he has been locked up. Mental illness? Nonsense! Menace to society, that man.'

Ashok Bhave, Prashant's nephew, stood at the receiving end. Ashok was an autorickshaw driver, but his licence had recently been seized due to his relationship with Prashant. 'We don't want you too to go around smashing vehicles into innocent people,' he had been told when his licence was seized. Since then Ashok had become obsessed with his uncle's case.

Prashant Bhave, a bus driver, now faced the death penalty for knowingly ploughing his bus into pedestrians and killing ten people. The story went that his employer had refused to give him leave for an appointment with a doctor who was treating his mental condition, and Prashant had gone on a rampage out of frustration and anger.

Prashant's lawyer had been pleading insanity, but the judge was having none of it. As far as he and the media saw it, Prashant had gone on a killing spree simply because he was denied leave. There was nothing more to be said.

Ashok had collected the clippings of every article on the incident and also tried to talk to as many people related to the case as possible. He had even attempted to speak to the doctor Prashant was seeing at the time of the incident, but the doctor refused to give him an appointment.

He remembered his uncle as always being a bit troubled and becoming seriously unpredictable only five or six years before, at which point Ashok's family had forbidden him from meeting Prashant too often. Maybe it was because it was forbidden that Ashok was even more drawn to him. Prashant had always been kind to him. He was disturbed and erratic, but never came across as someone who was capable of such a terrible thing.

Ashok had gone to meet Prashant after his arrest. Seeing him in a state of delirium in prison, dazed and confused, compelled him to find out why things had happened the way they did.

'Do you still feel angry?' Ashok had asked Prashant in prison.

'Angry? No, no. I feel good. They give me medicines so I can sleep,' Prashant had slurred.

He had seemed helpless, lethargic. 'Was his mind conscious but also somehow beyond him when he drove the bus into all those people?' Ashok wondered. 'Does madness come on like an uncontrollable rash that refuses to go away? You know it is your own skin, but also alien in some way?'

Ashok decided to meet the prison doctor to find out what was wrong with Prashant. He had not met him yet because he was scared to approach the prison authorities. But now, when nothing else seemed to give him any clarity, the prison doctor seemed like the only answer. His mind raced with the questions that he needed to ask. Why was there so much anger in Prashant? How were they treating his condition? Why had he been so incoherent when Ashok saw him last? And finally, the question that he really wanted an answer to: is madness like a hideous, uncontrollable rash?

He spent a week planning his questions and mustering his courage. On the day he felt ready, he reached the prison as soon as visiting hours began.

The prison official said that the doctor was not in.

Ashok was prepared for the resistance. 'My uncle is very sick, sir,' he pleaded with the official. 'I really need to know if he is okay.'

'Do you think the doctor has the time to talk to idiots like you?'

'Please just ask him once, sir. Please do me this kindness.'

The official appreciated his submissive tone. He made a show of refusing to help, but finally agreed to go and find out. Ashok nervously clenched and unclenched his toes in his new shoes. This was the first time he was wearing them, so they pinched a little.

'Go, the doctor will to talk to you.'

Ashok did not expect such an easy victory and ran towards the infirmary before the official could change his mind. A guard languidly followed behind.

'What do you want to know?' the doctor asked while examining a file.

Ashok sat on the slightly rickety chair opposite his desk and said, 'I was hoping that you would throw some light on my uncle Prashant Bhave's case.'

'What is there to say? He committed a horrendous crime and is now paying for it.'

'Yes sir, but I was wondering about his mental state. How is he feeling these days?'

'All the prisoners are given medicines called antidepressants twice a day. They all need it. Being in prison is not easy. Make sure you don't end up here.'

Ashok cleared his throat. 'But sir, the last time I met him, he seemed to have been sedated. He was confused and incoherent.'

The doctor looked up from his file, annoyed. 'Sedatives are only given to violent convicts. None of these prisoners are on sedatives.'

Ashok hung on to every word that the doctor uttered, but it all rang hollow. 'What about his anger issues?' he blurted. 'They said that he went insane with rage when he committed the crime.'

The doctor got very agitated at Ashok's insistent tone. 'Look son, I don't have time to waste. I alone cannot be responsible for each prisoner's mental condition. Do you know how many of them there are?'

'I understand, sir. I was just hoping that you would be able to tell me a little bit about his state of mind.'

'What else am I supposed to tell you? I am a general physician. This is a prison, not a hotel. We don't have the luxury to bring in a psychologist here.'

'But . . .' began Ashok. Before he could finish his sentence, the doctor gathered his file and stood up, gesturing to the guard to take Ashok away.

Ashok was in no rush any longer, so he walked slowly with the guard walking alongside him. Prashant was a closed chapter for everybody. The doctor's words rang a death knell in Ashok's mind: 'He committed a horrendous crime and is now paying for it.'

As he stepped out of the prison gate, Ashok decided to give up on his quest. 'What was I looking for anyway?' he said aloud to himself. 'How can madness be compared to a rash?' He made up his mind to focus on finding a job. The little money he had saved up was swiftly running out.

Rammohan's Nightmare

I had been asked to write an article on the news that had stunned the country: a father murders his own daughters, aged three, five and six. But my interview with Rammohan was going nowhere. I pushed him a lot, perhaps even a little more than I should have, but Rammohan refused to engage. His large eyes were bloodshot and very tired, as if his unearthly rage had only just subsided, even though the incident had occurred many months ago.

'People try to protect their families. I don't remember anything,' was all he said in a quiet, choking voice.

I had no choice but to visit his brother instead.

The brother, Shivmohan, was more forthcoming. He offered me some milky tea. I refused. We sat on the ground under a peepul tree just outside their common family hut. 'Ramu would have been dead had I not returned home just

that second,' said Shivmohan. 'He was hanging from this
very tree and his legs were shaking violently. I dropped the
sack of rice I was carrying and lifted his legs to loosen the
noose, then Ramu reached up and untied the rope himself.
As he fell on the ground, I noticed the bodies. All three
girls were lying behind the tree with their throats slit.'

'Why do you think he killed his own daughters?' I asked.

'Who knows?' he replied. 'The doctor in the prison
spoke of some kind of mental disturbance. Had we known,
we would have taken due precaution.'

'What kind of precaution?' I asked.

'Why would we have let him anywhere near the children
if we knew that he was mad?'

'Do you believe him when he says that he does not
remember anything?'

'It is possible. Two days before the killing, he had been
muttering to himself. It must have been the madness
coming on.'

'Where was his son during the time of the murders?'

'He had gone to gather wood with his mother. It is good
that he was not here. Ramu has only one son. It would have
been terrible if he had killed him too.'

'It must be a big strain on the family – the loss of one of
the main earners,' I said.

'Not really. It's true that we have lost an earner, but we
also have fewer mouths to feed now.'

At this point, Shivmohan got a bit fidgety. I tried to bait
him by talking about how stressful it must be to try and put
together dowry money for three daughters, but he did not

take it. 'Everyone loves their children. Nobody wishes for such a thing to happen to them,' he said.

Finally, I asked if I could speak to Rammohan's wife.

'No,' he said. 'She is not well. She will not be able to talk.'

I knew I would not get any more information from him. It was time to go.

I decided to speak to the neighbours next, but only one was willing to talk. His name was Madhav Kumar and he lived two houses down from Rammohan's hut. Everyone in the neighbourhood dismissed me, saying, 'We don't know anything about that family,' but Madhav Kumar had waved at me and called me over. 'I would advise you to not go to their house too much,' he said.

'Why is that?' I asked.

'They do jadu-tona … black magic. Didn't you see the scary statue of Kali in their house?'

'I didn't go in,' I replied.

'I have only been once,' he said, 'on the day that the murders happened. The police and the panchayat were all over this neighbourhood that day. I caught a glimpse inside, and the Kali statue really caught my attention. It was unlike any other idol I have seen. Don't know why the police did not pay much attention to it.'

'Does the whole family practise jadu-tona or just Rammohan?'

'No, not Ramu. Only Shivmohan does it. The entire neighbourhood knows this. Ramu used to be friendly, but a few months before the murders he stopped talking to us. Shivmohan must have either wanted Ramu's share of the land or he must have wanted to get rid of the daughters to avoid any future dowry hassles.'

'Do you have any other proof besides the Kali statue? And how do you know it was Shivmohan, and not Rammohan's wife or some other member of the family?'

Madhav Kumar took offence at my question. 'I have told you what I know,' he said. 'If you don't believe me, then ask somebody else. Don't waste my time.'

In their world of overwhelming desperation and superstition, the idea that Rammohan's brother might have turned him into a zombie through black magic, compelling him to kill his own daughters to save the family the expense of three dowries, almost made sense in a strange way.

I went back to Rammohan. 'Does your family ever visit you?' I asked.

'Sometimes,' he said. 'I don't think they like to see me anymore . . . It is also very expensive to travel this far.'

'What did the doctor say about your condition?'

'He gave me some pills and told me they would help with the nagging thoughts in my head.'

'Did your lawyer present the doctor's report in your trial?'

'No, I don't think so. I did not understand anything. The lawyer never spoke to me.'

'It would have made a huge difference if he had presented the report,' I informed him. Rammohan shrugged lightly.

'Didn't your lawyer discuss with you and your family what he was going to say in court?'

'I told you, I have never spoken to him,' he said.

The next stop had to be the court-appointed lawyer, Narayan Lal.

'I have come to discuss Rammohan Singh's case,' I said, as I sat in the rickety chair facing the lawyer's desk. The ceiling fan squeaked noisily. Narayan Lal pulled out Rammohan's file and looked over it quickly, and then, like a doctor giving bad news, looked up and said, 'It's a very difficult case.'

'Rammohan told me that he did not understand the court proceedings; it was all in English and you never tried to explain anything to him. In fact, he told me that you have never even spoken to him.'

'This is ridiculous. You dare to come into my office and start accusing me like this?' the lawyer spluttered. Then, calming down, he added, 'Of course I have spoken to him. And even if I hadn't, I have everything I need to know right here in this file. We try to make sure that the prisoners know and understand everything, but there is no helping those who refuse to listen.'

'But sir, why would Rammohan say that you have never spoken to him?'

'Do you know what his crime is? Everything he says and does obviously does not have a logical explanation. The records show that he is mentally sick. Nothing he says is reliable.'

'You must have brought up the issue of his illness in court? Surely there is some scope for leniency there?'

The lawyer was a little taken aback, almost bemused, and took a sip of his tepid tea in an attempt to hide it. 'I cannot discuss these things with you,' he said. 'If you have finished your interview, I would like to get back to my work. Rammohan's case is only one of the hundreds I am looking at.'

'Please sir, I just want to know whether you brought up the fact that he is mentally ill in court.'

'The court knows everything. And the next time you want an interview, don't try to teach me how to do my job. Please leave now.'

I had no option. I picked up my bag and left. Later, I reviewed the material that I had gathered – definitely enough for a short article. But before wiping my hands of the case, I wanted to meet Rammohan once more.

One last time I walked to the cell. Rammohan was sitting in a corner staring at his hands. He looked up, startled, when the guard called my name. Morning light flooded the cell, but did not reach Rammohan's corner. I did not try to draw him out of the darkness; I think the light hurt his eyes.

Redemption

'THEY had hoped that getting you married to Surinder bhabhi would stop you from spending time with me. Then when the plan did not work, they started these dirty rumours about my meeting her behind your back,' Rana said.

'You really think so? Why do they hate you so much?' Manpreet asked in frustration.

'Because they can't understand why you love me so much,' Rana replied.

'They have to understand that family is not everything; finding a real friend is a blessing.'

————◦————

According to neighbourhood gossip, Manpreet and Rana were provoked to action because they were confused young men. The general opinion was that Manpreet could never understand why his family wanted to keep him and Rana apart.

The following is the way a few neighbours told the story (although we do wonder how they could have been privy to the more intimate details of the protagonists' thoughts and interactions). We were told that Manpreet and Rana were relaxing as usual near the tube well on Manpreet's family farm. It had been a hard day of work for Manpreet and he was carefully opening the parcel of parathas his wife had packed for him. Rana was happy to share his friend's lunch and was whistling the tune of a new film song. Manpreet's two brothers saw them from across the field and came towards them.

'Hasn't father asked you to stay away from this lowlife?' they asked Manpreet.

'What is it to you both?' retorted Manpreet.

'So along with your wife, you like sharing your lunch with him too then?' Manpreet's younger brother chuckled.

As Rana stood up to defend Manpreet, his elder brother hit Rana on the head with a sugarcane stick that he had been carrying.

'I hope you will see the light before father decides to disown you,' one brother said to Manpreet before leaving.

'They think I will abandon my dear friend for a paltry inheritance,' said Manpreet, gritting his teeth in rage, as Rana tried to regain his balance.

In both their minds there were no options left anymore. Manpreet's bullying family had to be dealt with. According to the neighbours, the first thing the duo did was get

Manpreet's wife, Surinder, out of the way. She was innocent and did not have to go through what was to follow.

'Surinder bhabhi, you should go to your parents' house for a while,' Rana told her.

'Why?' she asked in her tiny, childlike voice. Women were not allowed to speak too loudly in their family.

'Because something big is going to go down in this house soon,' Manpreet said with a quiet, clear anger that Surinder had never heard in his voice in the one year that they had been married.

After sending her off safely, Rana and Manpreet planned meticulously for three days. They did not want to put off the matter for much longer; they felt they might not be able to go through with their plan if they waited. Manpreet's first step was to fetch his sword from a trunk in his father's room, where all the men of the family stored their personal weapons. Next, they took farm worker Lallu into their confidence and promised him a large sum of money in exchange for helping them with the attack at midnight.

———•———

The east wing of the large house belonged jointly to Manpreet and his younger brother, whose wife and daughter lay sleeping inside their room. The brother lay sleeping on a folding bed outside the room. The oldest brother lived with his family in the west wing of the house, and in a similar arrangement, his wife and daughter lay sleeping inside the room, while he slept outside. Manpreet's parents inhabited the centre of the house, and his three nephews slept on the terrace.

Rana positioned himself with his sword outside the window of the younger brother's room, and Lallu stood with his sickle outside the window of the elder brother's room.

Manpreet went after the younger brother first. He kicked him off the bed because he did not want to strike him down while asleep. Holding his slashed guts in his hands, writhing on the floor, the brother yelled, 'Run! Run!' to alert his wife and daughter. They tried to escape through the window, but Rana was waiting for them outside. Manpreet stabbed his brother once more to silence him, then moved on to his eldest brother.

The commotion had already woken him up and as he was running to their father's room to get his sword – Manpreet slit his stomach too. Lallu struck and killed his wife and daughter as they tried to flee by jumping out of the window. It was the parents' turn next. Manpreet slowly opened the door to their room. The stark contrast between the blood-curdling screams outside and the restful snores inside made him want to retreat to a corner and cry. But there was no turning back now. He killed them in their sleep.

Finally, he made his way to the terrace to find his nephews. All three boys had been sleeping on the same large mattress with thin sheets covering them. His eldest brother's two sons were still asleep, but the younger brother's son, eight-year-old Karan, had woken up, crawled out from under his sheet and hidden behind the water tank.

Manpreet climbed the last stair to the terrace and let out a violent, resounding yell. The two boys woke up with a jerk to find their uncle covered in blood. 'He looked like

Yamaraj, a monstrous god,' the neighbours said, even though none of them had been there when this happened.

Karan watched from behind the tank as his uncle hacked one of his cousins into two. The other boy jumped from the terrace and Manpreet jumped after him. Karan came out of hiding, and from his vantage point witnessed the two bloodthirsty men chasing his cousin through the field, cornering him near the tube well and doing to him what they had done to the rest of his family.

Manpreet had forgotten about Karan.

'All Karan wanted from then on was to avenge his family,' the neighbours said. 'To have Manpreet pay for what he had done.' He had to become the agent of justice for his family. The eight-year-old boy was the only witness in the case, and his account put Manpreet, Rana and Lallu behind bars.

Nobody in Manpreet's family had understood his love for Rana, but the police and the lawyers understood it even less. At first, Manpreet tried to deny and fight for Rana's sake, but Rana did not live for very long. He got killed while out on parole.

The neighbours told us that Rana's death triggered something unexpected in Manpreet – tranquillity. 'He stopped denying his crime,' they said.

The rigid routine in jail, devoid of any distractions, forced him to think. The drudgery of that kind of discipline brought him face-to-face with himself, and he slowly started to come to terms with the source of his madness. He loved Rana still, but he realized that he was not angry because his family did not understand their friendship. He was angry because he did not understand it himself – he had been angry with himself.

His tiny nephew, the youngest member of his family, had put him in jail, and Manpreet thanked him every day for it. Thus, unbeknown to Karan, he had also become the only source of redemption for Manpreet. Before sleeping every night, Manpreet would send up a prayer to god and to Karan. Nothing else mattered. As he followed the rules and tended to the prison's vegetable garden, he felt the fog in his mind lift little by little. He was atoning, slowly but surely.

We don't know how much of the neighbours' account of the events is true, but what we can say for sure is that today Manpreet is fifty years old and Karan is a strapping young man of twenty-eight with a wife of his own. Karan has never met Manpreet personally after the incident, but if he does, he will be surprised. Manpreet is the most loved inmate the prison has ever seen.

One of us recently mentioned the death penalty to Manpreet. 'I guess I would be happy to die now,' he told us with a smile. 'I have clarity. What more can life grant me.'

Rukhsar's Love

WHEN she finally had a little time, Rukhsar sat on her narrow prison bed and opened the letter addressed to her. It was sent by Adil Qureshi, a name that she did not immediately recognize. The letter ended with, 'I have always looked up to you. Please let me adopt Salman, so that my wife and I can give him a good life.'

It brought back memories, and memories were her enemy.

In a hot, crowded street of Barabanki, as Rukhsar made her way back home, jostling past vehicles, people and animals, she saw a man in a tea shop watching her quietly. A handsome man with a thick moustache, sitting alone on a plastic chair. All her prettier cousins – Abida, Shabana,

Bilquis and Shehnaaz – were with her, but he was looking her, as though hiding behind her plainness was beauty that only he could see. She knew then that she would do anything to keep him looking at her like that forever.

It did not take long for her to track him down. Samir worked as a cycle repairman at the local tyre shop. He was not very educated, but that did not matter; she had enough education for both of them. Her father had insisted that she study for a postgraduate degree.

After meeting Samir, Rukhsar's banal existence became tinged with a heady euphoria. His adoration was a potent secret that buoyed her above her family's jeers directed at her increasing age and diminishing marital prospects.

She once caught Samir glancing at a few modern-looking girls with short hair and decided to go to the hairdresser and get herself a fashionable bob. When she went home, all her cousins burst out laughing. One of them said, 'Do what you like with your hair, you still won't find a man ready to be tied down to that dark face.' Rukhsar did not mind. She knew that mixed with their contempt was envy; they would never dare to get their hair cut.

But now her hair had grown to look like that of all the other sixty-nine women in her prison dormitory. There was no difference at all now – all of them had dull, lifeless eyes and long, listless hair. The dormitory was full of beds, women and children. There was constant noise, but it was different from the noise that had filled her home, with her siblings and cousins talking over each other. This noise was more like a long-drawn screech piercing a deafening silence.

It was after one of her cousins got married that she had decided to broach the subject of Samir with her family. She had been tempted by the happy glow on her cousin's face during her nikaah.

'Have you lost your mind!?' her father had screamed. 'You have the gall to stand in front of your elders and talk about a love marriage!? He is not even from the community!'

Some had said that they would break her legs and others warned that they would get their machine guns out if she was ever seen in Samir's company again. She knew that these were not empty threats. She saw in their stony, suddenly alien eyes that if pushed, they would do the worst without a second thought.

There was only despair, and the panicked urge to find a way out of that despair. And then it happened. The nightmare. Three days later, they all died in the thick of the night. The throats of seven of her family members were slit, one person after the other.

How did it happen? Had she done it? Such questions were not important anymore. What was important was that it was all over for her. She had come to believe that she never deserved Samir's love in the first place. After all, her family had told her that no man could ever truly love her. It just wasn't natural. And now, they had paid the price for her arrogance.

She knew that the world considered her evil, so then what was this letter doing on her bed? How did this pure and beautiful gesture find its way into her extraordinarily ugly life? She did not believe in god, but for a fleeting moment she felt a warm, golden grace light her from within.

Rukhsar read the letter again. It began: 'I cannot understand how such a thing could have happened to you. I never got the chance to pay back the money you once loaned me for my college fees, but I want to repay your kindness by giving your son the childhood that he deserves.' With grace came the pain that she had managed to block for many years. Her insides, from her heart to her stomach, writhed in agony as she read the letter again and again.

Samir's affection had given her the generosity to help Adil in college. Something good did come out of their love after all.

'Why are you crying, ammi?' Salman asked, tugging at her salwar.

'I will take out your best clothes tomorrow,' replied Rukhsar, picking Salman up and seating him on her lap. 'Someone is coming you see you.' And she hugged him so tightly that he squirmed. He did not know that it would be one of the last times that she would get to hold him.

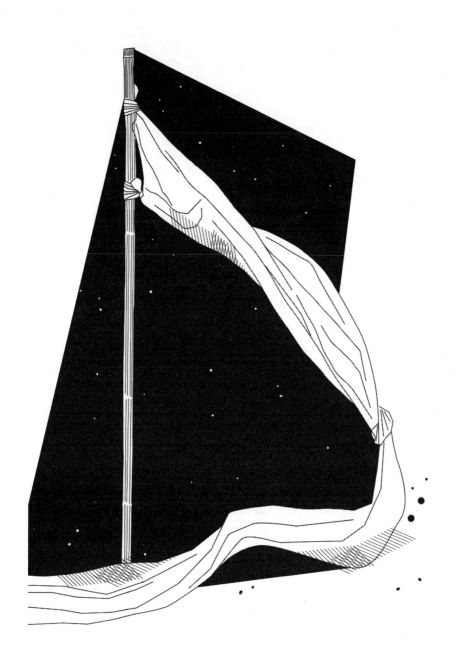

The Bogeyman

RANGANATHA'S friend said that they had met when Ranganatha was out of prison for a brief while. He said that Rangantha had told him everything that had happened to him personally in great and specific detail. I have presented here only a brief version of the friend's long story, which contained details that should perhaps be taken with a pinch of salt. None of these incidents have been corroborated by Ranganatha himself.

———•———

Even as Ranganatha rained blows on the security guard, something told him he would not get away with it. He ignored the warning and fled into the dark night, making sure that none of the money fell out of the cloth bags.

His friend told me that after his capture, Ranganatha was hung upside down from the ceiling and felt every blow of the righteous policemen. And without realizing it at the time, he begged for mercy in almost exactly the same tone and with the same expression as the security guard he had beaten a few nights before.

'No, no, no!' he cried. 'Please let me go!'

But the men did not listen. 'Tell us it was you!' they screamed, 'Confess!'

He felt ants crawling all over his body. 'The policemen must have poured sugar water on me to attract ants,' he later told his friend.

A few weeks after the beating, a chatty assistant jailer told him that he had become very famous. 'The newspapers are calling you the "heartless bogeyman".' The jailor read aloud with a smirk, 'Having robbed nine homes and killed seven people in the most brutal manner, from bludgeoning them to burning them alive, Ranganatha, the bogeyman, has gained household notoriety. Housewives in the entire state of Karnataka have started drawing their curtains at sunset. They scare their children with his name to stop them from lingering too long on the playgrounds.' He folded the paper, adding, 'You are a celebrity now. Our jail is honoured to have you.'

His friend said that Ranganatha was too weak to react to the assistant jailor's taunts. Every inch of his body still hurt from the police beating. In any case, he was completely consumed by worry for his wife and two daughters to pay attention to anything else. He could not sleep at night thinking about the kind of men that lurked outside his house, waiting to pounce on his family. But he was powerless to protect them from behind prison walls.

To add to the misery, the news channels continued to milk the story of the 'heartless bogeyman', airing some inane piece or the other every few days. It was while watching one such news item in the TV room that Ranganatha was introduced to Jagga.

'It seems you don't like to watch news about yourself,' Jagga said to him.

'All I want is to see my wife and daughters, which will be impossible if they keep showing things like this,' Ranganatha replied.

'Who is taking care of them now?'

'No one. We earn daily wages working in coffee plantations. How will she manage with just one source of income? I need to get out.' Apparently Ranganatha's voice broke as he said this.

'Did you get a lawyer?' Jagga asked.

'The lawyer came to me. He said he would take my case only because I had become famous. But how will he help me when he is convinced that I committed all the murders?' asked Ranganatha, looking straight ahead.

Jagga nodded with understanding.

'You know, my cousin told me that that madarchod lawyer even went to my house and molested my wife. I wish I could gouge his eyes out.' Then in a desperate voice, Ranganatha said, 'I need to get out.' He was quiet for a few seconds, averting his face to keep his tears a secret. In a tiny voice, he asked, 'What has my family done, tell me?

Why should they be made to suffer like this, starving and unprotected? Where is the justice in that?'

According to Ranganatha's friend, Jagga was shocked to see a grown man cry.

The heartless bogeyman's fame continued to spread, first in Karnataka and then across the entire country. And an increasingly thinner Ranganatha continued to toss and turn in his cell night after night, thinking about his family. Whenever he got time off his job in the prison's vegetable garden, he just sat in his cell and stared into empty space.

'He's lost it . . . maybe he's plotting another murder,' the other prisoners teased. Ranganatha had no time for them, because it was not murder that he was plotting.

Ranganatha's friend reported that by keeping to himself all day, Ranganatha had been able to observe chinks in the high-security prison. Thinking it better to have an ally, he drew Jagga into his plan. Early one evening, when both were sitting together in the TV room, the fan suddenly stopped and the TV shut down.

'I've noticed that there are very frequent power cuts here,' Ranganatha said to Jagga.

'It takes time for the generators to come on,' Jagga replied, waving off a mosquito.

'How much time?' asked Ranganatha, looking straight at Jagga.

'Around ten or fifteen minutes,' Jagga replied, as the meaning dawned upon him.

It was this window between the power outage and the generators coming on that was crucial to Ranganatha's plan. There was no fixed time for the next outage, so they had to be prepared to take advantage of one when it came.

'Have you noticed the bamboo poles holding up the banana saplings in the vegetable garden?' he asked Jagga, who had never been to the vegetable garden. 'They are very tall. We'll use them.'

His friend said that Ranganatha had worked in farms all his life, and he knew how to scale those poles. But Jagga had to be trained. Both got up at the crack of dawn before everyone else and trained together every day for three weeks.

The more difficult part was stealing bed sheets to make ropes. Both waited daily for the moment when the infirmary nurse left her post for a few minutes. Each time she stepped out, they managed to steal one or two bed sheets from the linen cupboard and hide them in their cell. They made long, sturdy ropes by tying one bed sheet to the other. Now all they had to do was wait for the next power cut.

It finally happened one night as everybody was getting ready to sleep. The assistant jailor was on his nightly round of the cells when suddenly the lights went out. He accidentally left the cell gate unlocked for a few minutes and went to check the fuse. Jagga was already asleep, so he had to be woken up. Shaking him excitedly, Ranganatha whispered, 'Quick! My wife and daughters are waiting for me!'

They pulled out the linen ropes from under their beds and slipped out without being seen. They climbed the low wall of the locked vegetable garden and found the bamboo poles to which they tied the linen ropes.

As they dug and pushed the poles into the ground against the compound wall, they noticed that the poles were a few feet short. But they had to take their chance. They began scaling the poles, fast and frantic. Sweat made their palms clammy and a bit slippery, but they kept going. When they reached the top of the pole, they caught hold of the linen ropes and climbed the rest of the way, finding tiny holes and nooks in the wall. As they hauled themselves to the top, the lights in the prison compound came on. They threw the linen ropes over the side of the wall and quickly climbed down.

The ropes weren't long enough, so they had to close their eyes and jump quite a distance.

'Then,' said his friend with a flourish of his hand, 'they ran through the undergrowth, leaving the white linen ropes shining in the dark, swinging behind them like giant victory flags.'

Every newspaper ran headlines on the audacious jailbreak of the 'heartless bogeyman'. The Karnataka police force was thoroughly embarrassed and the bogeyman's fame reached unprecedented heights.

———•———

According to the friend, Ranganatha did see his wife later. But when he got captured again, he wondered whether it did her any good. His family would continue to starve regardless. He told everyone he met later that as he was getting beaten mercilessly, a thought struck him: he had to stop being so emotional. The jailbreak was a useless stunt. He had to learn to think with his head – to be able to detach himself and watch from the outside. He remembered smiling at the thought with his bloody mouth, disconcerting the policemen a little. Then he felt the familiar sensation of biting ants. 'They poured sugar water on me again,' he thought as he drifted into blackness.

The Castration

THE mercy petition had been rejected. It was the television that informed Guru that his execution was set for the coming Friday. 'I knew I should have stayed in my cell today,' he thought as he left the TV room.

So many twisted crimes had been pardoned in the past that he was hoping the president would show some clemency in his case. As he walked back to his cell, Guru felt his anger rising in a tide of vomit. He swallowed and pushed it back in. He would need his anger to be able to use the rusty nail he had been hiding under his bed.

The case had taken long enough for him to have turned from a boy into a man. He had been given the time to feel the pain. He felt as if they had been toying with him, enjoying his screams before killing him off. So he decided to scream harder to entertain them till they flinched. He pulled down his pyjamas and pointed the rustiest end of the nail at himself.

He hacked parts of his body that he knew would make them look and then turn away in disgust. People panicked so badly at the enormous pool of blood that he almost laughed. 'The blood is too much for them – they like to cover the ugliness with a black cloth,' he thought as his eyelids got heavy.

'How did he do it!?' he heard the prison warden scream as he drifted into unconsciousness.

The last thing he felt was the tiny nail falling out of his bloodied hand.

———•———

As he woke up on bedding laid out on the floor in the corridor of the overflowing town hospital, a fellow prisoner being treated for an injury nudged him. 'So you got a stay order till you get better,' he said with a twinkle in his eye, as if that was all Guru had wanted. Guru dismissed him with a shrug. It was only when he saw the deputy commissioner of police (DCP) walking towards him that he really felt the urge to speak. He had met the DCP a few times and they had an understanding.

'You are a decent man, Guru. I expected better from you,' the DCP said.

'Why did they never speak to me, sahib?' Guru asked in a small voice. 'Why did the lawyers never ask me anything? Why was no DNA test done?'

The DCP was flustered. His constables yelled, 'Shut up! Is this how you talk to the senior sahib?'

Now that he had begun, he was not going to stop; not when they were going to kill him soon anyway. 'No one even told me when I was going to be hanged,' he said, disregarding the growing agitation on the DCP's face. 'I am telling you, sahib, they are all in it together because they are from the same caste – the girl's family, the lawyers, all of them.'

'Guru! You have been good so far, do not test my patience now,' the DCP warned embarrassed and stormed out with his troop.

Finally, tears fell from Guru's eyes. He had never let himself cry in prison, so now they refused to stop no matter how hard he tried. No one in that crowded hospital could have guessed that one of the patients there was crying for the first time in fifteen years.

He had been arrested at the age of eighteen for the rape and murder of a girl from his village. The village men had thrashed him and hauled him to the police station. Witnesses from the girl's family claimed that they had seen him dragging the girl away in the morning. Why had they not intervened and stopped him then? He found it difficult to mull over the events of that day.

Maybe it was because his life took such a sudden turn, but every time he tried to think about all that had happened on that day, his head would start pounding and his intestines would start to coil in on themselves. The only thing etched in his mind was how utterly helpless he had felt, sitting in a corner of a cell in the police station, trying to draw comfort by hugging his body close to himself.

Since that day fifteen years ago, he had only been trying to gain some understanding of the circumstances. He had begged his lawyer and the lawyer's assistant many times to bring in some kind of unambiguous scientific evidence. He had asked them to get a DNA test done or call in some witnesses who could speak on his behalf, but they continued to jabber in English and treat him like an illiterate child. He had even tried to speak for himself in court once, but the lawyer would not allow it. Guru was convinced that the family had killed their own daughter for some reason or another.

Doubts and uncertainties dogged him relentlessly – he had picked up that nail from the yard to rid himself of them; confirmation of the death sentence was simply an excuse.

As he sat in the hospital, tears collecting at one point on his chin, a nurse almost tripped on his outstretched leg. 'Sit up or I will send you back to where you came from!' she screamed, harassed and overworked. Guru ignored her.

He was very young when his father died. Since then, Guru had merely been drifting through life, staying sometimes with his mother and other times with his many siblings. Today, on the hospital bedding, he realized that it was only in jail, with death looming large, that he had really started to live. That did not mean that he had ever been happy in jail; no, he had been miserable. But he had learnt to think in jail. He had learnt to ask questions only when there was no one left to answer them.

The tears dried on his face as he watched the dirty ceiling fan turn uselessly.

He did not even remember the girl's face. The pain in his intestines never let him dwell on it long enough.

'Would it have been easier to let them kill me if I was sure of my guilt?' he wondered as he dozed sitting up, drained of blood and spirit.

राम
राम
राम
राम
राम
राम
राम
राम
राम

राम
राम
राम
राम
राम
राम
राम
राम
राम

The Life and Times
of Muskan Devi

ACCORDING to Titli Bai's statement, Muskan had snatched the gold chain from her neck and cackled, 'Give me that, whore!'

Titli said that as she lay drugged and bruised on the ground, Muskan made sure that her loud voice pierced some dark corner of her mind. 'She wanted the trauma to go deep . . . right into my nightmares,' she stated.

Tonight, though, it was Muskan herself who could not sleep. She pulled out her notebook from under her pillow and wrote 'Ram' on the page. She had started doing that out of necessity. The silence of prison life brought back such vivid memories that they threatened her sanity, so she wrote 'Ram' in her notebook every time she remembered something terrible. This one was the hundredth 'Ram' on the page.

No matter how anyone else might have judged it, Muskan firmly believed that her life as a bandit in the Chambal ravines had an intrinsic simplicity. You were either the victim or you victimized others out of revenge or necessity. But in prison, things got muddled. Because there was nothing to do, too many thoughts ravaged the mind so that the boundary between what happened to you and what you did to others slowly dissolved into one free-flowing experience of hell. And it did not matter whether you were the wretched victim or the victorious victimizer. The pain that she had inflicted upon Titli Bai now seemed as unbearable as the pain Titli Bai had put her through.

Unable to sleep, Muskan brought out the Bhagavad Gita from under her bed. The words lit up as she switched on the tiny booklight clipped on to the page. The Gita and the booklight were gifts from Faqir Chand, a ferocious dacoit with a Sufi bent of mind and her one true love.

The other women in the barracks snored in the darkness as Muskan read, once again, about how Krishna revealed himself to Arjun. She had been very young when she was kidnapped and taken to the ravines. She had learnt how to survive in that ruthless environment only by watching Titli Bai. Part of her had deeply resented her and part of her had simply observed and absorbed as Titli Bai unleashed her cruelty.

Muskan was beaten, dragged by the hair, starved and raped, and through it all she watched, learnt and plotted her revenge. She understood early on that as fearsome as they seemed, most of the men were to be used as props; you had to get close to one to end the other. While Titli Bai was heading the main gang with the sardar, Jabresh Yadav, Muskan decided to side with the rebel faction by marrying their leader, Mahendra Singh.

In a night-time guerrilla attack, they overthrew Titli and Jabresh.

As Muskan shifted on her thin mattress, she felt grateful. From sleeping under trees and inside caves in rocky ravines to sleeping on a firm but soft bed, the difference was unbelievable. She did not have much to go by other than the brutality of her previous life, so things that the other women sometimes took for granted felt luxurious to her. Not that she did not want to get out of prison – she was desperate for it – but it was endearing that people here took care of her when she was sick. Sometimes it almost felt like she was being treated like a child.

The chanting of Ram's name, the Gita and the prayers helped to keep her mind focused. There was no other way to make sense of everything that had happened in her life. Also it pleased everyone when she recited verses from the Gita – she seemed a little less terrifying then.

She had walked into the prison with a swagger. Every woman in the barracks had been afraid when she arrived. Unlike the ravines though, fear did not always work to one's advantage in prison. She knew that she had to change, and Faqir Chand had shown her the way already. A charismatic leader, he had triggered fear in the hearts of the comrades, but something almost close to affection in the hearts of the villagers. Even as they were arrested, Muskan saw that the policemen, despite themselves, were courteous to Faqir. His long, saint-like beard and the holy beads around his neck prompted respect.

Sitting in her bed in the darkness, as Muskan read the illuminated text of Krishna's twisted but sage advice to Arjun, she realized that both Titli Bai and Faqir Chand had been teachers to her. She now knew why she was drawn to the guru–disciple relationship between Krishna and Arjun.

Krishna had stressed the idea of karma – do that which is most just and appropriate in your particular situation. Muskan had done just that. She had always done what seemed most just in the ravines, although the idea of justice there was a little different from regular society. She behaved most appropriately in prison too – repenting and dedicating her mind to god. Always doing just what she had to, without complaining and without resentment. She had become a master of survival.

Titli Bai and Faqir Chand were both avatars of Krishna for her. They had revealed themselves to her, darkly and horribly in one case and benevolently in the other. Thanks to them she had survived everything – her kidnapping and her incarceration. But what about the death sentence? She wondered how she would survive the execution. Maybe Krishna would finally appear in his true form and save her in the nick of time – a breaking of the rope perhaps, or a sudden abolishment of the death penalty? Yes, maybe Krishna would intervene on her behalf as he had with Draupadi.

In that moment, with sleep eluding her entirely, Muskaan was overwhelmed with forgiveness, both for herself and those from her past life. It was time for a celebratory beedi. She pulled out a packet from inside her pillow cover. Sitting up on the bed, she lit it and took a deep drag. The tiny light of the beedi was brighter because of the darkness of the barracks. The smoke was strong and unpleasant, but no one woke up.

The Monster

'D ID you see the new prisoner?' Bansi, one of the inmates, asked his friend, Kallu, as they tended the okra patch in the vegetable garden.

'No, why?'

'You have to see him to believe it.'

Kallu did not have to wait long. He saw Dadu Aslam in the TV room that afternoon. The entire room went quiet as Dadu walked in. Dirty, long grey hair grew on half of his scalp, while the other half was bald. His face was so covered in ungodly scars that it was hard to tell where his nose ended, and his lips began and instead of eyes were just blank whites that stared back at the world. He was blind.

As he entered, he announced in a voice so loud that it seemed he was not at all ashamed – as if he was just presenting his essential self for all to see – 'My name is

Dadu Aslam. It is good to meet you all.' After making the
announcement, he made his way to a corner of the room
with the help of his stick and sat in silence.

Once the initial shock was over, one of the inmates
taunted, 'Allah must have taken his own sweet time to make
a specimen as beautiful as you.'

'Yes,' Dadu Aslam replied in his booming voice. 'My face
is disfigured. A motherfucker threw a lot of acid on me
some years ago. But this is not all – the acid melted other
parts of my body too.' Then he proceeded to lift his shirt all
the way up to reveal flesh that had fallen off the bone and
folded in on itself. One could almost smell the singed skin.
After giving everybody an eyeful, he pulled his shirt down
and sat in silence again.

'What an idiot,' one of the inmates said, as everybody
resumed staring at the TV.

Even though Bansi and Kallu were fascinated, they
kept well away from Dadu Aslam. Many years in prison
had toughened them up a little, but they were still famous
cowards. Neither had the courage to talk to him directly,
so they went to the assistant jailor to try and find out what
Dadu Aslam was in for. The assistant jailor was a chatty
man who had some regard for the inmates, and he especially
liked to engage with Bansi and Kallu because they amused
him.

'Gouged out a child's eyes hoping for an eye transplant.
Then strangled him and threw him in a pond. Dadu Aslam's
mother did it with him. She's doing life in the women's
prison,' he told them.

'I guess the operation was not successful,' said Bansi, chuckling.

The assistant jailor suppressed his laughter and ordered them both to return to their respective prison jobs.

One Tuesday evening, Bansi was in his cell praying to Hanuman and Kallu was watching TV alone. Dadu Aslam walked into the TV room and sat down next to Kallu, making him shiver a little, and asked in his resounding voice, 'Who is sitting next to me?'

'It's me, Kallu.'

'I can't hear Bansi's voice, Is he not with you?'

'He is praying to Hanuman.'

'Which god do you pray to?' Dadu Aslam asked.

'I don't believe in god. But I like Ganesh because I like elephants.'

'Tell me, Kallu, have you been given work here?'

'Yes, I work in the vegetable garden.'

Dadu Aslam ignored his reply and continued, 'I like to work with my hands. It is wrong for a man like me to be locked up like this. I could have made something of myself. I am an artist.'

'What do you mean "an artist"?'

'I used to make toys for children.'

Kallu mumbled a response, a little stumped by the irony of Dadu Aslam's crime considering his profession, but he knew better than to say anything out loud.

'I used to make beautiful toys,' Dadu Aslam said. 'The jailor refused to let me bring any plastic or thread with me, or I would have showed you.' Then with a sarcastic laugh, he added, 'The jailor said he could not allow those materials because prisoners could commit suicide using them.' As Dadu Aslam talked loudly, the TV room started to fill up. Bansi also returned from his cell.

Kallu did not want to be seen with the horrible-looking newcomer, so he moved a little away from him. Dadu Aslam sensed it and stopped talking.

Then, as the TV blared, Kallu whispered to Bansi that the big man made toys for a living, and they both laughed loudly. Dadu Aslam heard them. For many days after that, whenever Kallu and Bansi saw him, they would break into muffled giggles. One evening, as Kallu was getting ready to sleep, he noticed something hard under his sheet.

He lifted it to find the most delicate figurine of a baby elephant that he had ever seen. It had been made with soil, so it was the colour of dirt. It had enormous ears and a long trunk, and two big, beautiful eyes.

The Plastic-wallah

A large, brown sack lay at the gates of Central Jail. It looked like a sack of vegetables. The guard went up to it tentatively, expecting it to blow up any second, and gave it a little kick. It did not feel like a bomb; it felt soft and squishy. It gave off the smell of a thousand dead rats, and what he found inside as he opened the tie just a little was enough to make him want to quit his job. To hell with his wife and three children.

The police arrived immediately and the sack with a man's headless torso was hauled away for examination. They searched every corner of the jail and surrounding areas for the head and limbs of the murdered man, but found nothing. There was one policeman amongst them who claimed he knew who did it. 'I'm pretty sure it is the plastic-seller who sits at the bazaar,' he said to the inspector next to him.

'Who? How do you know that?'

'I was on my rounds a few weeks ago when he refused to give me the weekly tax. "How can you take money from us like this? It is not legal!" the bastard kept screaming, so I charged him with theft and locked him up. Since then he has always coughed up the money. But he also mutters something about wanting to give me a "bigger gift" one day. He says it politely, but he looks angry.'

'The bastard! We should go and ask him a few questions.'

The two policemen made their way to the bazaar, swinging their batons. They stood over the plastic-seller's wares for around twenty seconds, as if inspecting their quality. Then they casually asked him, 'What's your name?'

'Bheemnath Pandey,' he said, stiff and alert.

'So you think you are very smart, huh?'

'I don't think I am stupid, sahib,' replied Bheemnath with a twinkle in his eye.

This irked the policemen. They pounced on him from both sides. 'Come here, filthy bastard! You think you can get away with murdering an innocent man!?' they screamed as they dragged him through the bazaar all the way to the police station. Bheemnath's main concern was his plastic bottles and buckets. He hoped that his friend, who sold bangles next to him, would take care of them.

The police officials at the station were proud of their two colleagues for getting hold of the culprit and extended their full support.

'Tell us that you did it!' the policemen shouted as they threw blows and batons at Bheemnath.

'I don't know what you are talking about,' he kept repeating. But despite their many lashings, the policemen saw such a crazy glint in Bheemnath's eyes that they felt absolutely convinced about his guilt.

'I make an honest living, sahib,' Bheemnath pleaded. But the sparkle never left his eyes. 'I need to get back to the bazaar and make sure that no one steals my goods. I have procured them at a great price. I used to sell rice earlier, but ever since my crops failed, I have had to get into this expensive plastics business. Please let me go, sahib, I have to check if the stuff is safe.'

'Rice, eh?' one of the policemen said. Then he took the other policeman to a corner and consulted with him. 'Wasn't the body in a brown sack?'

'Did you sell your rice in brown sacks?' one of the policemen asked Bheemnath.

'How else am I going to sell it, sahib?'

That was all they needed. They took him to court saying that the sack in which the body was found was similar to the ones used by Bheemnath to sell rice. Luckily he was soon acquitted due to flimsy evidence.

The police continued to harass Bheemnath periodically and kept locking him up on some pretext or another. Within the next year, they found two more sacks with torsos lying in front of Central Jail. They were convinced of Bheemnath's guilt, but had no proof to nab him.

———•———

'They made me write this confession in the police station!'
Bheemnath screamed.

'Keep quiet,' said the judge sharply. 'This is not helping
your case.' Five murders in two years, without any
motivation other than to tease the police – the man was
beyond redemption.

The police stated that they had been called immediately
when the fourth sack was found in front of the jail. When
they lifted it, they saw a note stuck to the underside of the
sack. 'This is a gift for this town's police for taking care
of me so well. I have been intimidated, kicked around,
thrashed like a dirty animal by this able police force, and for
all that, I want to show my undying gratitude with this gift.'
The fifth sack had another note with the same text stuck
to it. Not only was the handwriting Bheemnath's, but the
murder weapons were found at his house too. Apparently
he strangulated the victims before chopping them up.

'They say I did the murders, but I was already in police
lock-up when they found the fifth sack. They are lying to
you, judge sahib.'

The trial was conducted in Hindi and English, so
Bheemnath understood only half of what was happening,
but he could not help interjecting whenever he understood
anything. The judge was irritated by Bheemnath's constant
interruptions. His crimes were heinous.

According to media reports, Bheemnath would first
befriend his victims, then after a few months, kill them on
the pettiest of grounds; for example, because they smoked
or drank too much for his liking. Worst of all, after finishing

the job, he would eat dinner with the dead bodies still in the room.

'This man is a menace to society and he seems remorseless about the suffering that he has caused. I believe that this man cannot be reformed, so I sentence him to be hanged till death,' the judge pronounced. A tiny chuckle was heard from Bheemnath's direction. The judge looked at him despite himself. Bheemnath's shiny, amused eyes haunted him for a month after that.

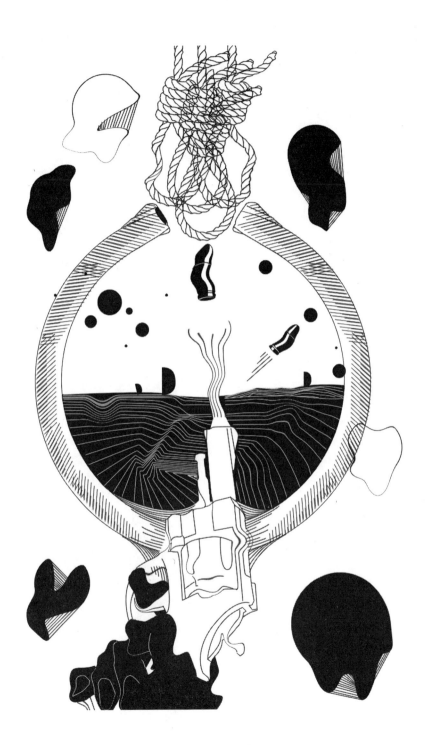

The Punished

THE following are the ramblings of an army officer who allegedly shot dead two other officers over an argument about identification documents. After waiting for twenty-five years as a death-row convict, he has now descended into madness.

'The real murderer ran away. I shot in the air just to scare them. I was at the scene, so I was caught.

'My name is "army guy". I have forgotten the name my parents gave me. I think it starts with a D.

'Twenty-five years waiting in jail, they tell me. I have gone mad waiting for death, they tell me.

'That which is born eventually dies. That which dies will be reborn. So there is no point in thinking. This is what the Geeta teaches us.

'I stood firm at the check post in the desert. They had no ID papers. How could I have let them go? I had pledged loyalty.

'The real murderer ran away. I shot in the air just to scare them. I was at the scene, so I was caught. Two good men died by those bullets.

'My mother too died some years later. She took my sorrow on her head. Mother is the greatest of all beings. I had pledged loyalty to my mother. Could not meet her before she died.

'You should not meet people if you do not have a point to make. It is a waste of time.

'One lakh sixty-two thousand.

'Anger comes after desire. Delusion comes after anger. Confusion after delusion. Confusion kills reason, and then man dies.

'Twenty-five years waiting in jail, they tell me. I have gone mad waiting for death, they say.

'I wish I could have seen my mother before she died. The government is my mother too.

'My wife is also a mother. She came to see me with my daughters when I was still alive. They can't come often. It takes money to travel to hell. They are all starving to death.

'It is all a story of karma. You are taken where you are destined to go.

'A man is his own best friend and his own worst enemy.

'The judge had no point, so he could not pronounce judgment.

'The real murderer ran away. I shot in the air just to scare them. I was at the scene, so I was caught.

'One lakh sixty-two thousand. The case has eaten it all. That is why they are starving. My mother, if she were alive, would have cried at the amount being spent.

'The fire that is essential – that died. That which had come out of my mother – that was fire.

'He will come when dharma dies and adharma reigns.

'The truth will always emerge victorious.

'If you cannot get me out of here, there is no point in talking to you.

'Twenty-five years waiting in jail, they tell me. I have gone mad waiting for death, they say.

'Mother is supreme. Mother can be made happy only through hard work. Not working hard is death to Mother. Could not meet her before she died.

'The lawyer could not argue well. He had no point to make.

'The real murderer ran away. I shot in the air just to scare them. I was at the scene, so I was caught.

'I did my duty well. The killer ran away. The protector was caught.

'They ate up one lakh sixty-two thousand.

'Passion is your enemy; it drives you to sin.

'The one who was born has been left in the darkness. The fire is dead.'

All attempts at getting a coherent answer about his condition were in vain. Finally, we gave up as a prison guard took him away.

The Real Parvathi

'BUT she was too shy to even touch the glass of milk that was offered. The prison warden had to insist for her to take even one sip,' Rakesh, one of the writers on the film, protested.

'Legend goes that the gang members starved most of their lives and could do anything for a bit of food. It will be much more exciting to show her grab that glass and let the milk dribble from both sides of her mouth as she drinks it,' said the director, visualizing the scene in detail.

'But ...' Rakesh interjected again, exasperating the actress, Mohini.

Mohini was the ideal lead and the director was overjoyed to have got her. She had agreed to do the documentary because she was eyeing the Critics Award. 'Don't you understand what is happening here?' she said to Rakesh.

'We are trying to externalize the character traits that we know exist inside her. Her apparent shyness hides a much darker interior; we are only bringing it out.'

Rakesh was silenced by what then seemed like a good argument, although it did bother him that some of the cases against Parvathi had not yet been proven. So the entire script was based on a lot of assumptions, but he told himself that it was just not possible to tell someone's story without making at least some assumptions.

As the film progressed, it became clear to Rakesh that Parvathi's character was turning out to be closer to what they thought she should be like rather than what she was really like. When the question of clothing came up, the director insisted that the actress bring out some sexiness in the character. 'Mohini, make sure that the sari does not cover too much,' he said. Mohini agreed with him.

But Parvathi was a very petite woman with an air of prudery about her. Rakesh remembered when the film crew was researching the workings of the women's prison, and how Parvathi had frozen when asked whether the prisoners were provided sanitary napkins. 'I don't know. I don't get my period anymore,' she had whispered, almost collapsing with shame.

'Let's at least not call the film "Parvathi's Gang", since the film is not really truthful to her life,' Rakesh nervously said to the director in private once.

'Don't be naive, Rakesh,' scolded the director. 'Have you forgotten what the gang did? They not only robbed those houses but also raped and killed the women inside. How could you be stupid enough to be influenced by her charade during that interview?'

In a particularly gritty scene of the film, one of the gang members was to be shown beating and raping a woman. Mohini, as Parvathi, was to help him by pinning down the struggling woman as the rape occurred. In real life though, Parvathi was too frail to have successfully pinned anyone down. The case was still unproven, so she might or might not have assisted in the break-in, but she could not possibly have physically assaulted anyone with any success. If Rakesh had to pick one moment where he decided for sure that he could not continue working on the film, it would have to be that day. 'I can't do it,' he told the director. 'I don't understand the objective of the film anymore.' He was promptly replaced, of course.

Being in between jobs and having many friends in the lower echelons of the film industry meant that he had the time and the resources to keep track of the progress of the film, even if it was from within his one-bedroom flat.

One day, he decided to go and meet Parvathi in jail again. He got access by pretending to be a part of the film crew. This time he noticed two little children, aged around three or four years, playing in the jail courtyard. 'Do you like to play with the children here?' he asked Parvathi.

'I am very tempted, but I try not to,' she said. 'They will leave soon and I don't want to get attached.'

He told her that the film was almost complete and that she should ask to see it before it was released.

'Why?' she asked quietly.

'Oh, you should make sure that you are happy with everything that is shown. Otherwise you can file a complaint.'

'Who will listen to me?'

'Who asked you to talk to the film crew?' Rakesh asked.

'DSP sahib had sent a note.' She meant the deputy superintendent of police.

'Then you should send a note to the DSP if you have a problem with the film.'

———•———

'Hard-hitting and spine-chilling,' read one of the reviews when the film was released. But Rakesh smiled to himself as he read the rest of the article, sipping tea in bed. A complaint had been sent to the deputy general of police by Parvathi, the alleged leader of the gang. Activists were asserting that the film was unethical how that it portrayed the gang members and should be banned.

Things came to a head when the opposition political party got involved. Demonstrations were held outside every screening of the film. Although Mohini received the Critics Award, she had to make an appearance on national television and apologize for the part that the film played in the social persecution of the gang members, independent of due legal process.

A few months passed and Rakesh got involved in the scripting of a different film. His job on this film was mostly to proofread for the main writer. One day, he received a phone call from the director of *Parvathi's Gang*. At first he was reluctant to answer the phone, but curiosity got the better of him.

'You put her up to it, didn't you?' the director snapped. He sounded drunk and Rakesh could hear music in the background. He seemed to be calling from a party.

'What are you talking about?' Rakesh asked.

'I know you went to meet her alone. She told me when we went to the prison to convince her to withdraw her complaint.'

'I was always uncomfortable with what we were doing,' Rakesh said.

'I had to pay good money to her family to get her to stop talking to the press.'

Rakesh was silent.

'I don't understand,' the director continued. 'Why are you so concerned about her? Does it not make you angry – the things they did? Why are you so worried about a realistic representation of that evil woman?'

Rakesh did not know how or what to say to him. He was quiet for a long time, but just as the director was about to disconnect in frustration, he said, 'You wanted to show pure evil in the film. But the truth is never pure – never just black or white. It is complicated. And there can be no justice without it.'

He cut the phone before the director could reply and got back to proofreading the new script.

The Study of a Murderer

I had been hired by a government organization to interview selected death-row prisoners held in the city prison. The objective was to provide brief studies of their circumstances, and I had to submit a completed report by the end of two weeks. I was apprehensive about the whole thing as I had never met a real criminal before, but the experience turned out to be less terrifying than I had imagined ... except this one case, which disconcerted and confused me a little more than the others.

His left leg shook violently – up-down, up-down – and he looked me straight in the eyes without blinking. Mohan Kumar's words were harmless, but his body language made me feel as though he was barely able to stop himself from attacking me. The guard was not too far away, so I managed to keep going with the interview.

'Why would my wife's family visit me in prison if they believed that I killed her and my children?' he asked me.

'What about your own parents and siblings? Do they visit you too?'

'I never want to meet my own people. But I am very close to my wife's family.'

'Can you tell me what really happened that night?' I asked. In retrospect, I should not have asked that question. There was no need for it, and it got me started on a fruitless path.

The speed of the up-down, up-down of his left leg increased and his fingers curled into a fist for a split second. I felt a chilling surge of dread. But he settled down soon enough. 'I can't reveal what happened yet. When I lost my family, it felt like I lost my legs. I was paralysed with grief. And now if I tell you who is to be blamed for all this, it will feel like my arms have been cut off too. No, no, nobody understands yet.'

He spoke coherently most of the times, but he would sometimes trail off and just stare at me. Maybe it was his intense agitation that made the prescribed questionnaire seem somehow irrelevant and made me insist on the particularities of his case.

'Are you willing to face the death penalty to protect somebody else?' I asked.

'Only in the supreme court!' he screamed, as if I should have immediately understood what he meant. His next few sentences made it clearer. 'There is no point in saying

anything in these lower courts. I will make an appeal in the
supreme court after these people pronounce their verdict.
Then the real events will be revealed for the whole world
to know.'

His lawyer had a different opinion. 'There is nothing
much to reveal. It is a botched case. According to the police,
he has admitted to the killing of his family. The police also
said that he raped his daughter as there was semen on her
skirt. But there was a significant delay in the examination,
so it could not be determined whose semen it really was.'

I had gone and met Mohan Kumar's lawyer, Ajith
Gopal, purely on impulse. I should not have done it,
but I felt compelled. Ajith Gopal had been a part of the
District Bar Association for nearly twenty years and had
contacted Mohan Kumar himself to take up the case. He
was forthcoming and quite talkative after I told him that I
worked for a government organization.

'So he confessed to the murders?' I asked.

'The police said that he did, but there was no judicial
confession.'

'According to media reports, his affair was the motivation
behind the murders.'

'Yes, he admitted that he had relations with another
woman. But I am not convinced that he committed the
murders to be with her. In fact, after his arrest, the woman
stopped talking to him.'

'Mohan insisted that there was a dark secret that he did
not want anyone to know yet,' I said.

'There is only one other thing that I can think of. The one
time that I met Mohan, he kept repeating that his youngest

son was not his own child. According to him, his wife had been sleeping with his work supervisor. But there is no way of proving this claim now that they both have been killed.'

'What was the evidence against him?' I asked.

'To be honest with you, there was no direct evidence that he committed the murders, only some circumstantial evidence. For instance, someone saw him on a bus bringing his daughters home from school on the day of the murders. I have great respect for the judge who presided over this case, but I do not think it is right to give the death penalty without any direct evidence.'

'This has been very useful for my work. Thank you for speaking to me,' I said and got up to leave. But the lawyer continued talking. 'I want to ask you,' he said, 'You are a young person ... what do you think of the death penalty? In Western countries they treat criminals in a humane manner, and their crime rates are lower than over here. You tell me, has the death penalty achieved anything?'

'I'm afraid my job stops me from commenting on this issue,' I replied before getting out of his office.

'My lawyer, Ajith Gopal, is working for the police. He wants me dead,' Mohan had said when I interviewed him, his leg shaking and his eyes wide and piercing. 'I am telling you, madam, they all want me to die in prison. I will reveal the truth only in the cupreme court.'

After having met Ajith Gopal myself, I could not understand why Mohan said the things that he had.

———•———

I failed to wrap my head around Mohan Kumar's obsession with 'the truth' and its eventual 'revelation'. Why didn't he reveal the truth to his lawyer? Was the lawyer somehow involved in the killing of his family? None of it made sense because the lawyer seemed to genuinely believe that Mohan Kumar should not be given the death penalty. It made no logical sense for the lawyer to be lying to him or to me.

Then there was Mohan Kumar's belief that his youngest son was the product of his wife's affair. Why didn't he tell me that? It couldn't be his big revelation, as the lawyer whom he claimed to distrust already knew about it. Maybe he had killed them because of the wife's affair, but how did that sit with the fact that he himself was having an affair? And after all this, how was it possible for his wife's family to still be close to him?

Mohan Kumar's arguments seem more and more untenable as I think about them now. It has become clear to me that his stories are deeply held delusions. Mohan Kumar is a man suffering from an untreated mental illness. Those who deal with criminals regularly would probably think nothing of all this, but to me it is shocking that a man who should be in a hospital is being held in a prison that really cannot deal with his condition.

I don't know what to do about it though. My report is only supposed to be a basic overview and there is no way of fitting it all in there.

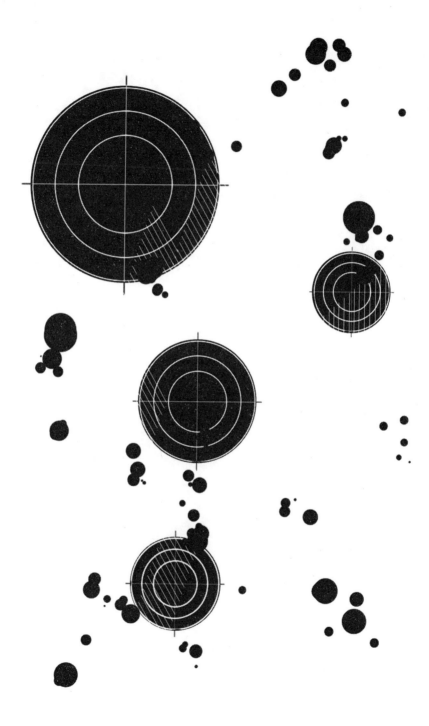

The Family Feud

ALTHOUGH Balwinder did not like his chacha, he was somewhat friendly with one of his chachi's distant nephews, Jaspreet. It is Jaspreet who gave me this written account of how Balwinder had tried to justify his actions to him. I don't know whether to believe this or to just chalk it down to Jaspreet's need for revenge, but here is his account of what Balwinder narrated to him:

> I went after Chachi as she tried to flee. She didn't really want to escape, having seen her family destroyed by the cold, precise bullets in my gun – all she wanted was to be killed too. It was pure instinct that made her run. She didn't get very far, and I saw pain and relief on her face as I pulled the trigger. The first three murders were instantaneous. I remember Chachi most clearly because

she gave me time to think when she tried to get away. But there's nothing to be done now.

Almost immediately I found myself in jail again. 'Why, Balwinder, why!?' my father and brother kept repeating. But they did not expect me to answer; they knew my rage.

My lawyer was a woman. She was exasperated. 'You were on parole,' she said. 'Why would you do such a thing?'

How was I to explain this to a woman? How can a woman understand the purity of the anger that hot-blooded men feel? That so-called chacha of mine was a bastard in more ways than one. He was the child of a whore that my grandfather had impregnated. It had to end like this.

He grabbed part of the land that rightly belonged to those of us legitimately related to the family. He probably plied grandfather with significant quantities of drugs to make sure that he willed it to him. The bastard did not feel any shame when he framed me for the rape of his own daughter. He made sure that my life would be over.

I had watched his daughter grow from a tiny tot to a woman. How could I have missed her when he insisted on tainting every auspicious occasion and family function with not only his own presence but also his three children? He did not care, no matter how many times he was told that he was not welcome. I never thought of his daughter as my cousin – she was only the granddaughter of my grandfather's whore – but how could I have raped a blood relative?

The lawyer had promised that I would be released as the charges against me were obviously a lie. But there was no way I could have lived a normal life after the shame of such an accusation. People would have pointed fingers, no matter what the court said.

So I did what I had to do as soon as I got parole. My family begged me to remain calm. Everyone in my family is well educated they like to follow the rules. But I only follow my heart. I took my pistol with me, though my intention when I left home was only to express anger. At the most I had hoped to beat up my chacha and send him to the hospital.

But seeing him at the dinner table, enjoying his life while he had ruined mine, made my blood boil. When he saw me, he smirked. He had the gall to laugh at me. Everything turned black in front of my eyes and I only saw my target. I had to shoot him.

Then I shot his two sons, who sprang at me from both sides. Chachi howled and ran, but not too fast. She wanted to be shot. She wanted it all to end. You could even say that the fourth murder was almost merciful. Their daughter was not in the house at that time or she would have been dead too.

Now I try not to think about it too much. I wake up early in the morning and do fifty push-ups and sleep at night humming my favourite film songs. My whole family comes to visit me sometimes. They love me despite what I have done, or maybe deep in their hearts they are glad that I have erased that blot on the family name. Not only my father and my brothers, but even my father's brothers – my real chachas – and their families come to see me.

They all gather here and chatter about this and that, just like they did at home. It makes me feel special that they adjust their plans to spend time with me. They probably start from home like they are all going on a picnic. It makes me feel like I'm getting married or something. All the boys in my family have completed their graduation and got married. Everyone except me got their special days. I did not even finish school. At least this way everybody will always remember me.

My father has been hit the hardest because of all this. He is trying his best to save me, but it is a waste of time. I did commit the murders – who can deny that? But I would like the judge to remember what that fraud chacha did to me. His plan was to destroy not just my life but the respectability of my entire family. I took revenge – that is all I did. Sometimes it is difficult to think through the consequences of your actions. You can get so swayed by emotion that you forget that you will later be held accountable for everything you say or do.

I see Chachi in my dreams. I wake up screaming in the middle of the night because I can feel the fear I saw on her face just before I pulled the trigger. I feel bad for the girl who came home that night to find her entire family murdered. I wish I could ask for forgiveness, but that will not do her any good. I am just glad that she was not there in the house during that hour.

I try not to think of the end too much. Death will come anyway; whether it's now or later does not matter anymore. Dharti Ma gave me the strength to pull the trigger that night, and she will also give me the strength to withstand the punishment. I am not afraid of death.

According to Jaspreet, Balwinder had written all this down on a piece of paper and handed him his 'confession' because he considered him a friend. There is no signature on the paper, though. I do not know how seriously to take it.

The Trap

VIJAY'S shrivelled mother sat on a cot outside her tiny hut, sipping tea. She had just washed herself at the community hand pump after three days, so she looked even more prune-like, with her thin, grey hair sticking to her scalp. Her cataracts were so severe that her eyes resembled the muddy grey shade of her torn sari.

A young man passing by said to her, 'Drinking tea early today, amma?' She looked away without replying. She felt that her brain had turned grey too, making her nervous when people spoke to her. She usually drank some tea late in the evening to stave off hunger till the next day, but today, thanks to a neighbour's charity, she was celebrating her full stomach with a little early brew.

She had lived all her life in that small hut. Her parents had given her away in marriage to a poor farmer when she was a child, but her fate had been sealed even before she crawled out of her mother's womb. At sixty, she looked ninety, and with her husband dead and her sons and daughters making their own mistakes far away, she hoped that she had paid her dues.

Her mother used to tell her that she had bawled at the skies when she was born. Her own youngest boy, Vijay, had cried inconsolably too. She was to live and die in that hut, and had accepted her destiny unquestioningly. But Vijay had gone away to the big city when he was just a young boy, hoping to free himself from a life of poverty. He had tried to spread his wings only to discover that it was impossible to escape their cage.

Sometimes she even forgot that Vijay still existed. But when she did remember him, her heart twisted into painful knots. She was glad that she could never sustain one thought for more than a few minutes.

———•———

If there was one good thing about prison, it was that he never went hungry. His belly had grown larger in prison than it had ever been before. Vijay would smile sadly at the meal he received and remember the tedium of chopping vegetable after vegetable for the family that had employed him as a cook.

Somehow, even though he was used to being kicked around, he deeply resented the slaps and pinches of the wife of his employer. He did what he was asked in such complete silence and endured the abuse with such stoicism that the woman had grown a little bit afraid of him, which made her lash out even more.

'We want it now!' the children of the house would scream day after day for their pre-dinner snacks. Vijay had burnt himself with hot oil countless times while hurrying to get the samosas and the pakoras to their plates on time.

'Quick! Quick!' their mother would shout at him. Vijay believed that the woman secretly relished it when he burnt and cut himself in the process.

Then the noisy eating would begin. As he watched the kids chomp and slurp down their food, he would fantasize about pushing them into the big dry well in the garden. He hated his employers for treating him badly. He hated them for trapping him in that horrible cook's job. He had wanted to be a driver, not a cook, but they withheld big chunks of his allotted salary so that he wouldn't run away. The fact that he had managed to free himself from his village but got trapped again in the city made his blood boil.

He remembered his mother many times in those days. She was the only gentle soul he had come across in his life, and she had taught him enough to be able to tell the difference between good and bad people.

And then the fire happened. It was the middle of the night as he watched the giant angry flames take over the entire house. The cage was burning to the ground. The screams from inside the house reached him in the garden and he was scared. As he was the sole survivor, the police were bound to blame him. The well was his only option. He climbed down the rope and squatted on the dry floor of the well, trying all night to guess at the goings-on above with the help of the sounds that trickled down to him.

After around three hours, it struck one of the policemen to glance into the well. 'There's a man in here!' he called out, and after descending into the well with the help of a rope, he grabbed Vijay by his shirt. A couple of policemen pulled the two up and Vijay was caught. He tried to convince them, but they refused to believe that he had not started the fire.

With every crack of a police baton on his body, Vijay shed a tear. The burning of the cage was a joke that the universe played on him – a trick only to remind him that there was no escape. A lot of scenarios ran through his mind as he was beaten. Instead of hiding in the well, he could have alerted the neighbours or he could have just run to the police station and told them of the fire, but no one would have believed him to be innocent. All situations would have led him to the same spot – hanging from the ceiling with batons beating down on him.

That week, as the police beatings continued, he eventually accepted his fate. He did not know that his mother had accepted hers a long time ago, when she was just a child.

———•———

'Don't come here again,' Vijay's mother had firmly told the journalist who wanted to interview her after her son's arrest. 'I am an illiterate fool. I do not know how to answer your questions.' She even refused the food that the journalist had offered. Not having eaten at all the previous day, she was very tempted to accept it, but she knew she would be obliged to think and answer in exchange for it. The pain of thinking about Vijay was unbearable, and she had trained herself to never let her mind wander there for too long.

Now, five years later, she sat sipping an early tea in the sun, oblivious to the fact that Vijay's mercy petition had been rejected. She had encouraged her forgetfulness to keep him out and had succeeded. These days, she could not even remember to wash herself every day, let alone recall that her son had been sentenced to death.

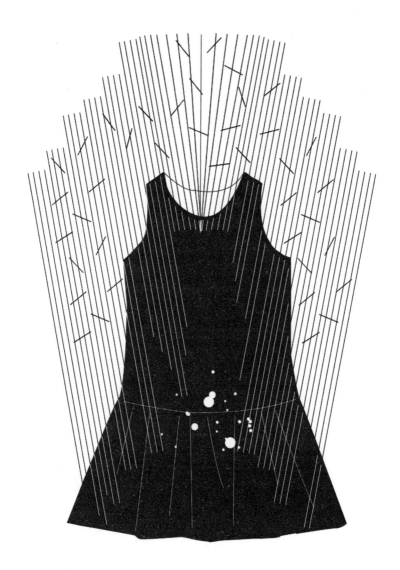

Whatever Happened to
Sadhna?

THE activist laid out all the versions of the interviews she
had taken so far. Her office was dark with no windows,
and despite the fluorescent tubelight she had to turn on the
table lamp to be able to read clearly.

Sarju's Version

Sadhna would run and hide behind her mother every time
Ramesh returned home at night. The whole hut would
start smelling of cheap liquor. But his wife, Sangeeta, was
so afraid of Ramesh that she would force Sadhna to come
out from behind her and greet her drunk father to calm
him down.

Ramesh is a well-known gunda – a gangster. He has
been to prison many times for theft and for beating up

people. He beats Sangeeta too. He thinks that I was
having an affair with Sangeeta, but it was she who always
flirted with me. I was caught in between the two of them.

Ramesh's mother, who is my mother's sister, brought
me here with the hope of getting me a good job. But
when I started work as a motorcycle repairman, she
struck a deal with my employer and started receiving a
big portion of my salary. But what could that old woman
have done? Her own son squandered all his money on
drinking and gambling. Ramesh even started asking me
for drink money and would beat me up if I refused.

Sangeeta treated Sadhna badly paid her no attention.
You couldn't even tell that she was her daughter. She let
her run around with a runny nose, dirty and hungry. One
night, the neighbours called us for a Satyanarayan puja.
It was a big event and there were many people there.
Ramesh got drunk early. The paanwala said that he had
seen a girl in a blue frock with Ramesh. It had to have
been Sadhna. They did not even find a full body in the
field; it was half eaten by wild animals. They could not
even tell if it was a boy or a girl.

Ramesh had built a network over the years and knew
some of the policemen well. They beat me, took some of
my blood and put it on the body to prove that it was me.
They have given me the death sentence, but it is Ramesh
who should rightly be here.

Ramesh's Version

Don't repeat what Sarju said. It is all bullshit! That
bastard raped and murdered my four-year-old daughter. I

would kill him myself if I got a chance. He confessed to the police too. Now he says that he was beaten and forced to make that confession, but that is nonsense. His blood and semen were found on the body.

He is a strange man – always very quiet. Something is wrong with him in the head. I thought I could trust him because he is my cousin, but he turned out to be a snake. My mother brought him here to help him get a job and earn some money, but instead of being grateful he started an affair with my wife. I have caught him sleeping in the same bed as Sangeeta several times. He did not even spare my daughter. I wish I had thrown him out of my house sooner.

He used to be around Sadhna all the time. He was always too keen to play with her. He could listen to that child's long stories for hours on end. I should have known to be careful right from that time. Sadhna was a lonely child. Her mother never took good care of her. That is why she became an easy target for Sarju. First he went after my wife, then he went after my daughter. If the court had let him go, I would have risked everything and killed him with my own hands.

Ramesh died of a gunshot wound soon after this interview. It is unclear whether he killed himself or was murdered by a rival gang member.

Sangeeta's Version

My little daughter has been killed. What do you want me to say? Who can I blame but myself? My life is empty now. Oh, my little girl! Where have you gone?

There were many people at the puja that evening, but I made sure never to take my eyes off my little Sadhna. I had bought her a special blue frock that she was wearing that evening. I let her go with Sarju because I trusted him. That bastard!

She used to talk to herself a lot. Sometimes I still feel like I will find her in that blue frock talking to herself in some corner of the village. But I know that that will never really happen.

I never thought that he was this kind of a man or I would have never left her alone with him. Some villagers come to me and ask why Sarju only thought of a four-year-old girl as an option when there are so many women in the village. They don't understand that some people are just evil – there is nothing more to it.

I don't know what to do anymore. My husband has gone mad with rage. There is not even one minute in the day when he is not drunk. Sarju is in jail. There is no one to earn money for me and my mother-in-law. If things continue like this, we might even starve to death. There is a chance that I might marry again. But what will my mother-in-law do? The old woman has a sad ending written in her kismat.

After Ramesh died, Sangeeta and her mother-in-law were indeed left destitute and homeless.

The Lawyer's Version

There were reportedly so many people that evening at the Satyanarayan puja that the girl could have gone with anybody. There was another lawyer looking at the case initially. I took charge only towards the end, but by that time the damage had been done. The truth is that there is only circumstantial evidence against Sarju. There is absolutely no direct evidence that he has committed the rape and murder. I don't think it is right to give the death sentence based only on circumstantial evidence.

Sadhna had been missing for a whole night and the body they found in the field the next day had already been mangled by wild animals. There was just no way of telling that it was Sadhna's body. In fact it was in such a bad shape that the doctor could not even tell whether it was a boy or a girl. Apparently it was just hands and legs. How can you give the death sentence in such a case?

The judge did not listen to anything and had already made up his mind. He is notorious for doling out the death penalty. His name is Mithiles Mishra, but in the lawyer community we all call him 'Merciless Mishra'. There were blood and semen samples on the body that were recovered, but Sarju kept insisting that the police took those samples forcefully. The judge argued that it is just not possible to force semen out of anybody.

The Satyanarayan puja that night had attracted a very large crowd. Who knows what happened to the child?

———•———

Thwarted in her attempt to make sense of the case, the activist exited her office. The sun was beating down disconcertingly, so she missed a step and tripped a little.

Author's Note

Iwant to begin by drawing attention to the important work carried out by Project 39A, NLU, in facilitating a discussion on the death sentence. Their work helps us gain an understanding not only of the ethical aspects but also the practical realities of the ways in which the justice system in India works. I would also like to thank Project 39A for the research material they made available to me for this book.

This collection hopes to provide brief vignettes into the lives of death-row inmates, but I do want to alert the reader to the fact that although these stories are based on real lives, they are not direct transcriptions of the prisoners' experiences. Despite the significant material gathered by Project 39A in the form of interviews with the prisoners, their families and lawyers, only a limited amount is known about the inner lives of the convicts. Accordingly, I used the glimpses that the prisoners allowed into their worlds in Project 39A interviews along with media reports and my authorial imagination to construct these narratives. The names of the prisoners, people associated with them and the specifics of their crimes have been modified and obscured to protect their identities. Owing to the limitations mentioned above, no story in the book can be considered an entirely factual representation of any one prisoner's life. Nonetheless, I hope that together the stories will provide an important perspective on the prisoners' experiences as a whole.

I believe that people are products not only of their own histories but also of the communities within which they are rooted. Accordingly, I have always maintained that justice can prevail only when criminals cease to be viewed as existing in vacuums, entirely separate from the everyday life of a society. Yet, when I began my research on the death-row inmates, I was appalled at how challenging it was for me to dissociate the convicts from their offences and see them as people with lives beyond the crimes they had committed. The crimes were so monstrous that it was difficult to grasp that the prisoners could have stories to tell from before and after the moment of the critical act. I admit to this to underline that my intention is not to simply condemn society for making assumptions about death-row inmates, because I too shared the same emotional instinct at first. Having said that, it is also our duty as evolved human beings to judiciously suppress our first instincts in order to arrive at informed and well-rounded conclusions

– my attempt in writing this book is to help the reader to do just that.

I would like to take this opportunity to address the related question of media reportage. A free media is the mainstay of any progressive society. It wields such power that its responsibility cannot be overstated. Therefore, tempting as it may be to capitalise on the audience's knee-jerk reactions of disgust and paranoia, I would urge the media to extend sensitivity towards both the victim and the accused when reporting a difficult crime. The media can influence social judgement and subliminally pronounce verdicts even before cases are tried, and a widely circulated opinion fuelled by fear and a need for revenge can distort our understanding of the world around us. My hope is that in demystifying the convicts, this collection of short stories will have an antithetical effect to that kind of hate and scare mongering.

Writing in English was a complicated but necessary choice. The complication arose from the fact that the English language is a definite bane in the lives of some of the prisoners. It is a well-known fact that a majority of death-row inmates are from impoverished backgrounds and are not very well educated, and even though very few of them understand English, their legal hearings are at times carried out in the language. The problem with English in India is that we can neither do with it nor without it. Since it is not taught as a primary language in the government sponsored schools accessible to most people, it is difficult to shake off its colonial and elitist associations, but without any knowledge of English, it is impossible to engage in a dialogue across the many cultures that make up our country. These stories needed to be in English not because they seek an audience of any particular milieu, but because their scope would have been regionally limited had they been written in a different Indian language.

I would also like to address the issue of authenticity – the question of whether I should be allowed to tell these stories without having any direct experience of prison life. I wrestled with this question a great deal, because while these stories are based on real prisoners, they are dramatized versions of their lives and have required me to envision characters in situations I have never actually been in. But instead of being limiting, I found the process to be enlightening and humbling. I discovered that once I pushed aside my conditioned response of thinking of the convicts as somehow being less than or different from regular human beings, it became easier to imaginatively walk in their shoes. After all, even though the situations we are put through in life differ radically based on external circumstances, our humanity ensures enough similarities for us to find some connection with each other, however tenuous that connection may be. If there was no way for one person to relate to the story of another, all artistic endeavours would be rendered futile. In telling these stories as an outsider, I am doing exactly what I hope for the readers of the book to do – to open themselves up to the experiences of a group of citizens who have been so silenced that they have become almost unrecognisable as human beings to the rest of society.

Having said that, I don't want these stories to generate a sentimental or a simplistically sympathetic reaction from the readers either – none of the stories in this collection attempt to play down the magnitude of the prisoners' offences. In fact, sympathy in certain situations can be a treacherous thing because it can blind us to the bigger picture. It is after all the immediate sympathy we feel for the victims of these crimes that precludes us from seeing the convicts as fully human and deserving of legal rights and due process in the first place. Instead of sympathy then, I would prefer if the stories evoke a sense of understanding in the readers – an understanding not merely instinctual and sentimental, but one that is measured and has the capacity to include both the victim of a crime and the accused in a crime. More than anything, my attempt in these stories is to contextualise the convicts not to justify their crimes in any way, but simply to show them as people embedded within their social systems, just like all of us are.

The power of a story is inherent in the opportunity it provides the reader to open up to experiences that may otherwise seem remote. Stories, unlike theories and abstractions, rouse our intellect via our emotions, and in doing so can help us understand people and ideas that are alien to our worldview. In this collection, my attempt is neither to sway the reader one way or another with regards to the death penalty nor to justify the acts of the death-row prisoners in any manner. Instead, my effort is simply towards reminding the readers of the commonalities between them and the convicts as human beings. I believe that if we as a society take on the onus of punishing with death, the least we can do is get to know the ones we punish a little bit better.

Finally, I would like to thank Aparajita Ninan for her beautiful illustrations. I also want to express my gratitude to Apoorva Mundoor for his unwavering support through the ups and downs of this project.

About the Authors

Jahnavi Misra is a writer, researcher and filmmaker. She has a PhD in English literature from Durham University, UK, and her current research work focuses on the ways in which feminist philosophy interacts with feminine sexuality. Her short stories, creative nonfiction pieces and academic work have appeared in various print and online journals over the years. Her interests in filmmaking lie mostly in animation. Her latest animation film is about the death penalty in India and has won accolades in multiple film festivals around the world. She can often be found enjoying a horror film with a glass of wine and a slice of pizza.

Project 39A is a criminal justice research and litigation centre based out of National Law University, Delhi. It is inspired by Article 39A of the Indian Constitution, a provision that furthers the intertwined values of equal justice and equal opportunity by removing economic and social barriers. These are constitutional values of immense importance, given the manner in which multiple disparities intersect to exclude vast sections of our society from effectively accessing justice. Using empirical research to re-examine practices and policies in the criminal justice system, Project 39A aims to trigger new conversations on legal aid, torture, forensics, mental health and the death penalty.